"The worst crime is not to tell the truth to the public."

Winston Churchill,
Prior to World War II, as
he tried to warn England and
break Government and news media
silence about the massive Nazi
military buildup.

The Reason For This Book

"We are not just a little bit behind the Russians, we are devastatingly behind them ... I think the time has come when we have to quit fooling around and trying to lie to the American people."

Senator Barry Goldwater
March 5, 1982—in a letter
to President Reagan

For years Americans have been told and have believed that the reason for four decades of Russian military build-up is that the Soviets believe they must match American military strength in order to be safe from nuclear attack by the United States.*

Over and over again, year after year, as the Soviet Union modernized its ballistic missiles and added massive numbers of nuclear warheads, as Russia developed and stockpiled enormous quantities of chemical and even biological weapons, and as the Soviets planned and prepared a nationwide anti-ballistic missile defense system, the American news media subtly 'sold' the idea—and we accepted it and still accept it—that the U.S. and the U.S.S.R. are equally menacing.

Over and over again, year after year, regardless of ever-more naked reality, we have been told and we have believed that the military power of both nations is roughly equivalent.

And over and over again—starting even long before America lost her own supremacy—we have had thoroughly impressed in our minds and enshrined in the pantheon of popular perception that both sides would be able to destroy each other in the event of nuclear war.

This book shows with incontrovertible facts why these are

---

*Throughout this book the terms "Russian," "Soviet Union," "Russia," "Soviet," etc. are used interchangeably primarily for reasons of style and notwithstanding the objection to equating the country, Russia, with its Soviet dictatorship or the Russian people with the aggregation of subjugated nationalities comprising the 272 million "citizens" of the Soviet Union. Cf. Aleksandr Solzhenitzyn, "Misconceptions about Russia are a Threat to America." *Foreign Affairs*, March, 1980.

I

four of the most dangerous myths and misconceptions ever accepted in our Democracy. The text reveals the full truth that the Soviets have far surpassed our country in military power and *already* have achieved overwhelming military superiority over the United States which may soon *prove decisive*; a superiority whose details are almost completely unknown to the American people including those they trust to warn them—the Congress, the staffs of Capitol Hill, network television, the major newspapers, and even the White House.

The book reveals, furthermore, the real *purpose* and possible employment of Soviet military supremacy, the degree of which is shown to be increasing unabated with every passing month. And, of special significance to every American, the book tells the saddening story of our own actions and inactions which have made possible and speeded the growing potential for our gradual demise as a free people and independent nation.

The authors are acknowledged experts on U.S. and Soviet military affairs. Over time, they became increasingly distressed that the full facts of the scale and direction of the Soviet military buildup seemed never to be assembled into one clear, simple-to-read presentation so that the complete implications of that buildup could be seen clearly by all Americans. From government files, from expert testimony before Congressional committees (virtually none of it ever publicized by the U.S. news media), and from countless other sources here and abroad, they have put together in one volume what is truly a story of tragic proportion.

In measured and dispassionate tone, their work explains:

- Why the policy selected 25 years ago by the United States to prevent Soviet nuclear attack, Mutual Assured Destruction (MAD), is now known to have been based on a flawed premise.

- Why, instead of leaving *their* entire population, plus *their* land-based missiles and bombers unprotected from nuclear attack *as we have done*, the Soviets have already invested well over 100 billion dollars to protect their people and their military from any missiles we might launch in response to an attack by them.

- Why the American military response to such a Soviet surprise attack would now be so weak it would cause no more (and probably far less) casualties to the Soviets than they suffered during World War II.

II

In so doing, the authors expose the reasons for the discomforting and corollary truth that the Soviets can now destroy *all* of our land-based missiles *on the ground*, right in their silos, whereas we are powerless do the same to theirs.

They describe how the Soviets can obliterate at least three-fourths of our 239 old, slow-flying B-52 bombers *on the ground* and knock down the 50 or so which might survive with more than 3,200 MIG and Sukhoi interceptor aircraft and 13,800 high-performance surface-to-air missiles.

In detail, the authors explain further that in order to neutralize our entire submarine missile force the Soviets are ignoring the Anti-Ballistic Missile Treaty by building large scale illegal battle-management radars for guiding their SA-12 interceptor rockets, which reach ballistic missile speed of 12,000 MPH in seconds and thus give the Soviets the power to destroy our submarine missiles 100,000 feet in the air at the edge of space, long before our missiles could reach their targets. Also uncovered are revolutionary new Soviet capabilities for detecting and thus destroying submerged U.S. missile submarines and the related reasons that led Eugene Rostow, former Director of the U.S. Arms Control and Disarmament Agency, to dismiss the value of our submarine fleet as a fully effective deterrent to war.

These and the many other facts carefully amassed and newly revealed in this publication, if examined with an open mind, force us to recognize that the capability of our country to deter a Soviet nuclear attack by fear of American retaliation could soon be entirely gone. The data and analysis presented make abundantly clear the exact extent of the dangerous military imbalances which have arisen in the span of only a few years and why even Dr. Henry Kissinger has warned that *the years facing us now* will be "a period of vulnerability such as we have not experienced since the early days of the Republic."

Are Soviet leaders taking international political advantage of our growing vulnerabilities? Will they take even greater advantage in the future?

In this book you will read, probably for the first time, the many statements by Soviet leaders which prove that the *real* purpose of the massive Soviet military buildup is not self defense but to gain an awesome strategic advantage and with it the crucial international supremacy and crisis leverage derived from the unquestioned ability to fight and *win* an intercontinental war.

You will learn the harsh fact that while the American people have been sold the notion that nuclear war would totally destroy both nations, Russia has focused its entire national effort, sacrificing everything except the most basic needs, to achieve the capacity to *survive* a nuclear war and to defeat any combination of opponents. You will learn, quite simply, why Soviet capabilities, both offensive and defensive, will very soon be so overwhelming that the Soviets could realistically believe, as President Reagan recently warned, that they were in a sufficiently strong position to say with confidence, "We can destroy you. You cannot destroy us. Bend to our will . . . or face devastation."

If such an ultimatum is given, either directly or (as is far more probable) tacitly and gradually, it will come from a tyranny that treats total war and suppression as a natural part of history.

On this very day, the Soviets have approximately *five million* of their own citizens incarcerated in slave labor camps, living and working under conditions of unbelievable hardship and suffering. It is estimated that 500,000 men and women die in these camps every year.

On an even larger scale, and indeed in every important sense, *all* of the Soviet Union is itself a vast prison with the equivalent of 20 KGB Divisions and 30 MVD Riot Divisions—more than one-half million specially-selected troops—deployed simply to control a people who are consulted neither on their own future nor on the high stakes of international confrontation.

And in open warfare, the Soviets are even more inhumane.

Consider this recent (unreported) report from the Department of Defense:

"We have no evidence to suggest that the Soviets are concerned about civilian casualties resulting from their use of chemical weapons. Evidence from Southeast Asia and Afghanistan shows that *civilians have been the specific targets of chemical weapons.*"*

---

*Throughout the text, as in this quotation, any emphasis added is that of the authors unless otherwise indicated.

IV

Consider also that in 1980, soon after the invasion of Afghanistan, the Soviets conducted lethal chemical and biological tests against men and women tied to stakes in target areas at the gigantic Shikhany Chemical Test Range located southeast of Moscow and that such tests are apparently continuing.

Consider finally that the Soviets have 14 chemical weapons production facilities operating at full capacity. (The U.S. has none.) They have 8 biological weapon production facilities. (The U.S. has none.) And the Soviets have an estimated 150 intercontinental ballistic missiles for *global* delivery of these horrifying weapons.

These facts should be known by all Americans in order to understand the modes of thought of our opponents and the implications for us of their new and growing power. Yet not one person in a thousand in this country is remotely aware of them.

At the outset, the authors furnish easy-to-read "box scores" which give the stark figures on actual Soviet military strength versus that of the United States at the beginning of 1985. What you will read in concise format is so startling that you may find the information disclosed hard to believe—you almost certainly will not want to believe it—but the cold figures demonstrating our severe vulnerability are taken exclusively from official sources and public records.

Later in the book you will learn why nearly all Americans are unaware of these facts. You will learn why virtually all in the U.S. news media have ignored them and why United States officials do not discuss them. You will learn how all of us, as citizens in a democracy with a duty to the future, share responsibility for the tragic, incremental erosion of our strength and how *the rhetoric of our times does not match the reality of our forces.*

But of greatest importance, you will learn, *unfiltered and unabridged*, the grisly implications of the new strategic reality now dawning for our country and the Free World . . . and for you, your family and children.

We who asked that this book be written welcome the opportunity to have it distributed because the time has long passed for all Americans to know the complete truth, to see its whole meaning, to reject the myths, and to act . . . because in the final analysis the survival of our American Democracy is not a duty of the government or of the news media, but is, instead, the ultimate responsibility of the people.

This book is a project of
The Defense and Strategic Studies Program
University of Southern California
Los Angeles, California 90007

SOVIET MILITARY SUPREMACY

THE UNTOLD FACTS ABOUT THE NEW DANGER TO AMERICA

Quentin Crommelin, Jr.
David S. Sullivan

Contents

Notice: In accordance with the contractual obligations of the authors, this book has been reviewed and cleared for publication by the Central Intelligence Agency.

Introduction

by
Steve Symms of Idaho
United States Senate

First as a Member of the House of Representatives and now as a Senator, I have observed at closehand as Congress time and again makes incorrect and often dangerous decisions on matters vital to American security and freedom. Congress does so because of an astonishing disinterest in the truth of our current strategic inferiority and because of an equally cavalier disregard for the evidence of Soviet aggressive intention toward the Western Democracies.

But the unvarnished truth is rarely popular in politics, and nowhere is that more true than in matters concerning American security. With ever rising federal deficits, few voters want to hear that military spending must be increased to counter Soviet military might, and most politicians, therefore, understandably far prefer the political safety of inaction and acquiescence over the political dangers of action and leadership.

It has happened before. During the years preceding World War II few leaders chose to suffer the political risk and consequence entailed in warning the Free World of the reality of the Nazi military buildup.

The analogy today is all too clear. While the Soviet Union engages in the most massive military buildup of all history, most Western politicians still insist on minimizing the significance of these activities. They conceal the truth from the public and delude themselves in the belief that their inaction is somehow justified in the cause of world peace.

The theory goes that Soviet aggressive behavior can be modified by ignoring it in public, by persuading and negotiating in private, and by keeping the American people in a false feeling of security through denial or concealment of the facts. These omissions and distortions are rationalized as necessary in order to preclude any "inconvenient" or "dangerous" public political demand for Western rearmament.

The authors of the book you are about to read do not accept that theory. Nor do I. Our Republic and the other remaining democracies thrive on truth just as the Soviet Union thrives on falsehood. Certainly, there can be no justification for withholding from the public basic essential information concerning American strategic vulnerability, when the issue, ultimately, is our national survival itself.

In this context, unfortunately but obviously, I cannot discuss information still restricted by security classification; however, I do feel at complete liberty to say in a general sense that based on knowledge obtained in an official capacity I am deeply impressed by the high degree of accuracy of the data the authors present. Yet there remains *even more* information the American public should have and should have soon. The material given here will hopefully begin that process.

For that reason and for many others, I recommend this volume, to you and to all citizens, as a thought-provoking assessment of the current strategic imbalance and of the new implications of Soviet military supremacy for Western freedom, both internationally and at home.

The picture painted is unpleasant to contemplate, but we must understand the facts as they are, not as we might wish them to be, if we are to remain free.

Steve Symms
United States Senator
Washington, D.C.
February 22, 1985

Authors' Note

In 1980, reliable polling data uniformly indicated that a majority in the United States believed that American defenses had become significantly *inferior* to the military power of the Soviet Union. The obvious accuracy of those polls was reflected in the subsequent Presidential vote of the same year by which a President the public viewed as weak on national defense—Jimmy Carter—was enthusiastically replaced by one the public viewed as strong—Ronald Reagan.

Today, reliable polling data indicate that a majority believes the United States to be *equal* or *stronger* militarily than the Soviet Union.

The majority was correct in 1980, but it is our belief that over the ensuing four and a half years the majority has been led dangerously astray.

We believe, and believe we can demonstrate, that the decline in the relative military power of the United States has been continuous and that it is, in fact, accelerating. We know of nothing tangible since 1980 that has materially reversed the trend then apparent, notwithstanding millions of empty words to the contrary in countless campaign speeches of the 1984 election.

Almost no Americans realize that, because of Congressional action and inaction, defense spending under President Reagan is *far below* the levels even President Carter thought were necessary for our safety, nor are they aware that Congress has *already* cut defense spending *far below* the *total* cumulative five-year increase that President Reagan urged when he entered office in 1981. The Reagan buildup occurred only as a proposal on paper which Congress refused to implement, yet most Americans believe the exact opposite because the facts have never been effectively provided to them—perhaps since the information is considered "insignificant" by those who would be most embarrassed by its widespread knowledge.

In writing this book, we have sought to dispel these and other grave misperceptions with the facts, chiefly those that have been untold or underemphasized by the government and the media. As a major part of that process, we value remembering our national past to gain a current perspective on our character as a people and to see more clearly the on-going direction and true degree of our decline.

History does not repeat itself precisely, but history does teach the precise inevitability of change. We hope, therefore, that a public better informed about the nature of the changes which have already occurred can mold those which are surely coming to allow our country to continue in the safety and freedom with which it has in the past been blessed.

In that regard, many Americans living today can still well recall that only forty short years ago their country enjoyed preeminent military superiority over all potential opponents and indeed over every conceivable combination of other nations. As had been seen as proven fact during World War II, the people of continental America in 1945 were inaccessible to direct attack by any enemy, and the United States Government was effectively immune to any form of military coercion anywhere on the globe. On the contrary, America was itself in a unique position to impose its will on a turbulent world in which peace could have been established exclusively through the unprecedented magnitude of American strength.

Yet America did not choose to use its position of unchallenged dominance and did not launch a preemptive war against the worst long-term threat to peace, the Soviet Union, even though Russia had breached its solemn commitments to allow self-determination in Eastern Europe and had initiated an obvious program of protracted aggression.

America did not act when it had the power to act because Americans, besides having an inbred national desire for peace, also have an almost inexplicable national preference for waiting until the eleventh hour to correct even the most threatening conditions.

Yet, in some sense, that peculiarly American trait can be understood. With a remarkable history of unparalleled advancement achieved while adopting precisely an attitude of procrastination, Americans have developed an entrenched faith, buttressed by national experience, that *nothing* is ever too late to correct and that the game can always be won on the last down. That positive conviction has been, seemingly, justified by our record.

Leaving crucial matters to the very last has repeatedly characterized our response to virtually every social and economic ill. Yet we are the richest, the most free, and the most egalitarian society on earth. Leaving matters to the very last characterized our belated and ill-prepared entry into both World Wars. Yet we decisively prevailed.

But now our success is becoming our downfall. Now our

over-confidence and blind faith in the future promises not the deserved rewards of optimism but the just deserts of folly.

In this book, to the best of our ability, we present the bitter facts documenting the most systematic military decline of a great power in the history of mankind. We have not relished the task, but we have felt it to be necessary because Americans who so much cherish the land where they were born are entitled to know her peril.

The summaries you are about to read offer a "box score" or "snapshot" of the existing military force structure of the Soviet Union and the United States at the beginning of 1985, all developed from official U.S. Government sources.

Obviously, the figures presented are not unchanging and only represent the situation for the present moment. In fact, tremendous military production and research momentum favors Russia and will assure further growth in the asymmetries disfavoring the Free World for at least the next decade ... almost without regard to what action is taken by the United States.

Although the data given could easily lead us to conclude that America can never recover from its present dangerous inferiority, *we do not believe that to be the case.* Our future as a nation holds promise and hope beyond imagination—but only if the President and Congress act decisively, at once, and in concert—with the support of an American public which has been told the truth.

Accordingly, in reading the following box scores we ask you to keep always foremost in mind the thought embodied in these words spoken in 1935 in similar circumstances by Winston Churchill:

"Never must we despair, never must we give in, but we must *face facts* and draw true conclusions from them."

Numbers That Count

The Facts of Soviet Military Supremacy

"For my part, whatever anguish of spirit it may cost, I am willing to know the whole truth: to know the worst, and to provide for it."

Patrick Henry,
in 1776

BOX SCORE NUMBER ONE

ON-LINE STRATEGIC NUCLEAR FORCES

United States	Soviet Union
Intercontinental Ballistic Missile (ICBM) Launchers (including SS-20s and SS-16s)	
1000	1,850
Heavy ICBM Launchers	
Zero	820
Ready ICBM Warheads	
2,100	9,300
Ready ICBM Warheads capable of destroying ICBM Silos*	
Zero	7,070
Total ICBM Warheads (including reload, SS-20, stockpiled, and covert missile warheads)	
2,100	20,200
Ballistic Missile Submarines	
35	101
Intercontinental Range Submarine-Launched Ballistic Missiles (SLBMs)**	
Zero	596
Intercontinental Range SLBM Warheads	
Zero	2,000
Cruise Missile Submarines***	
3	220
Sea-Launched Cruise Missiles*** (Nuclear armed)	
12	575
Intercontinental Bombers	
239	650
Total Intercontinental Delivery Vehicles (*excluding* Soviet reload missiles and reserve forces)	
1833	3500
On-line Ballistic Missile Throw-Weight**** (Millions of pounds)	
4.4	12.4
Predominant Age of Systems (years)	
15	5 or less

Note: Basic sources are the Department of Defense and the Arms Control and Disarmament Agency. Removed from U.S. forces are the 80 B-52 D's, the 54 Titan II ICBMs, and the 160 Polaris Submarine Missiles which have been or are being rapidly deactivated. The overwhelming Soviet missile reload and refire capability is *not counted* in this box score of on-line forces (except to show total ICBM warheads) but is reflected in the next box score which deals with strategic nuclear reserve forces. SS-20 Launchers and a limited number of ready SS-20 warheads *are* counted for reasons stated in Box Score Number Two. However, *not counted* are approximately 1000 MRV nuclear warheads on the Soviet SS-11 Mod 3 ICBM *nor* are the warheads in over 125 Soviet "test and training" launchers which house missiles carrying approximately 675 *additional* nuclear weapons. Moreover, there is credible evidence that the Soviets plan as many as five rapid reload and refire salvos for each ICBM launcher whereas the data assumes only one reload per Soviet launcher. American submarine-launched ballistic missiles (SLBMs) are much less capable than most Soviet SLBMs in terms of range, accuracy, and yield; thus, the U.S. advantage in *numbers* of SLBM warheads (about two to one) should not be allowed to mislead (as is often the case) since the American disadvantage in SLBM *capabilities* is enormous. In fact, most Soviet nuclear warheads (including those comprising the truly incredible Soviet numerical advantage in the vital category of ICBM warheads) are on the average *ten times* more powerful in yield than U.S. warheads, and they are more accurate.

*The 1650 U.S. Minuteman III warheads may have some capability against Soviet ICBM silos, but Soviet missile mobility and improvements in silo hardness and defenses make highly doubtful the effectiveness of these U.S. warheads for that purpose.

**SLBMs which can be fired from home port at intercontinental range equivalent to that of ICBMs.

***The number of U.S. SSN-688 attack submarines armed with nuclear capable cruise missiles probably will increase (notwithstanding a Congressional ban on current funding) but the total planned deployment will be only a small fraction of the number of *already* deployed Soviet nuclear armed cruise missiles which can attack U.S. coastal regions where, unlike the USSR, more than 50% of our population, industry, and infrastructure is located. Moreover, the Russians are in the process of deploying off our coasts the SS-N-21, the SS-N-24, and other extremely long range cruise missiles which can hit targets *anywhere* in the United States when launched by submarine from sea. Unlike their slower U.S. counterparts, some of the new Soviet cruise missiles are supersonic and correspondingly more difficult to find and shoot down with a highly limited number of American interceptor aircraft.

****The eight-million-pound throw-weight advantage in favor of the Soviet Union *does not include* Soviet reserve or reload/refire missiles but only counts on-line ready to launch forces. The United States has no reload/refire missiles and no operational reserve. If Soviet reload/refire and stockpiled missiles are included, the Soviet nuclear throw-weight advantage approaches six to one.

BOX SCORE NUMBER TWO

RESERVE STRATEGIC NUCLEAR FORCES

United States	Soviet Union
ICBM Launchers with ICBM Reloads (including SS-16s, SS-20s, and SS-11s)	
Zero	1850
Modern Stockpiled and Reload ICBMs	
Zero	3350
Modern Reload ICBM Warheads (including SS-16s and SS-20s)*	
Zero	9,300
Stockpiled Older ICBMs	
100	1500
Fractional Orbital ICBMs (SS-9 Mod 3)	
Zero	18
Rail-Mobile Modern ICBMs (SS-24)	
Zero	100
Road-Mobile Modern ICBMs (SS-25)	
Zero	200
Covert Intercontinental Bombers (Bear-H Bomber with Air-Launched Cruise Missiles, ALCMs)	
Zero	50
Covert Strategic Air-Launched Cruise Missiles (ALCMs)	
Zero	150
Total Reserve Strategic Launch Systems (Reload, Covert, and Stockpiled Systems)	
Zero	3,700

Note: Sources are Department of Defense, U.S. Arms Control and Disarmament Agency, and Congressional and public reports. In its strategic nuclear reserve, the Soviet Union has *an order of magnitude more* strategic nuclear delivery vehicles and warheads than are counted in their on-line forces which, as seen in Box Score Number One, already greatly exceed those of the United States. The United States does not have a strategic nuclear reserve nor *any* unacknowledged launch systems. In this analysis, the SS-20 is counted as an ICBM since its range probably exceeds the 5500 km ICBM range definition agreed in the unratified SALT II treaty. (The International Institute for Strategic Studies gave the SS-20 a range of 7,400 kilometers.) To include the SS-20 in the lesser tactical or illusory "theater" category would be misleading since it has clear strategic potential because of its range, accuracy, and yield as is evidenced by the inclusion of all SS-20 regiments in the Soviet Strategic Rocket Force Command and by the mixing of SS-25 ICBMs in SS-20 launcher regiments. The best evidence that the SS-20 is an ICBM is the fact that it has been operationally fired on an azimuth directed at the United States. Moreover, the range of the SS-20 can easily be increased by loading two warheads instead of three, and its practical intercontinental capability can be enhanced, even with three warheads, by Siberian basing, for example at Anadyr. The missile is mobile.

*These data assume only one reload missile for each SS-20 launcher. Public reports indicate that current intelligence estimates reckon that the USSR plans up to five reload missiles per SS-20 launcher which, if correct, would increase the number of modern Soviet reload and covert ICBM warheads from 9,300 to an actual planned total of at least 11,700 in the near term.

**Projected. Deployment of the SS-25 in operational regiments is underway at the Yoskar Ola and Yurya Missile Complexes in the Central Soviet Union. The Soviets are developing or deploying four new types of ICBMs: the SS-24, the SS-25, the SS-X-26, and the SS-X-27. U.S. analysts estimate that the SS-X-26 will have a five ton payload with extreme accuracy to a range of 7,000 nautical miles. The SS-X-26 and SS-X-27 will both be larger than the already gigantic Soviet SS-18 which is *seven* times larger than the U.S. Minuteman III. The SS-18 force of 308 on-line missiles (*excluding* reloads) carries total ready warheads with explosive power *greater than* the *entire* U.S. ICBM and SLBM force combined. Meanwhile, Congress has stalled production of the U.S. MX ICBM, which is one-half the size of the SS-18. The first MX cannot be operational until 1987 or later in any event.

BOX SCORE NUMBER THREE

ANTI-NUCLEAR STRATEGIC DEFENSE FORCES

United States		*Soviet Union*
	Surface-to-Air Missile Launchers (SAMs for Continental Air Defense)	
Zero		13,800
	Primary Anti-Ballistic Missile Launchers (GALOSH and ABM-3)*	
Zero		100
	Secondary Anti-Ballistic Missile Launchers (SA-5, SA-10, SA-12)**	
Zero		3,500
	Modern Interceptor Aircraft (To intercept intercontinental bombers and cruise missiles)	
42		3,200
	Air-Defense Radars	
117		7,000
	Civil Defense	
Effectively none		Massive and nationwide
	Operational Anti-Satellite Systems	
Zero		4 system types
	Satellites for Detecting Submerged Submarines	
Zero		2 system types
	Anti-Submarine Warfare (Attack) Subs	
99		280
	Percentage of ICBM Warheads Defended by ABMs	
Zero		Up to 33% and growing

Note: In early 1984, the United States was developing an F-15 Fighter/Anti-Satellite System (ASAT), but Congress blocked testing and deployment. This action coincided with the Soviet proposal to ban ASAT testing to prevent the development of any U.S. capability which might threaten their Submarine detecting satellites or their command and control and strategic targeting satellites.

*The Soviet ABM-3 is a highly advanced ballistic missile interceptor system which is rapidly reloadable and carries two types of high-acceleration interceptor rockets per launcher. One rocket, the SH-08, intercepts at relatively low altitude (above 50,000 feet) and the other, the SH-04, at higher altitudes in outer space. In March, 1984 the Soviets resumed testing of the SH-08 at Saryshagan to improve the agility and maneuverability of the weapon. The ABM-3 is being deployed initially to defend the Soviet capital and adjacent ICBM launch sites. Notwithstanding the ability of the ABM-3 and SA-12 to down our ballistic missiles, the Administration eliminated funds for the development of anti-ABM penetration aids for the Trident SLBM and for the MX and Minuteman ICBMs. 100 ABM launchers are either operational or being modernized near Moscow.

**The SA-5, SA-10, and SA-12 rockets are frequently armed with nuclear warheads and can also be used for air defense against bombers as well as, in the case of the SA-10 and SA-12, against low-flying cruise missiles. The SA-12 is openly acknowledged even by the Soviets to be designed to intercept U.S. ballistic missiles in flight.

BOX SCORE NUMBER FOUR

TACTICAL NUCLEAR FORCES

United States	Soviet Union
Tactical Nuclear Delivery Aircraft	
Land Based	
451	6,800
Tactical Nuclear Missiles	
100	800*
Net Tactical Warheads Planned	
for Withdrawal or Withdrawn from Europe since 1981	
2,400	Zero
Net Tactical Warheads Added	
in Europe since 1981	
Zero	2,300

*This figure is a rough approximation of the currently deployed old SS-12, Frog, and Scud missiles and the newly operational SS-21, SS-22, SS-23, and SS-C-4 (Ground Launched Cruise Missile-GLCM) systems fielded by the Soviets since 1981 (all of which systems are concealed and camouflaged), but it does *not* include the reload missiles for these systems or any of the up to 1200 on-line SS-20 warheads which, as previously noted, are more properly counted in strategic systems on the basis of range and warhead yield and because SS-25 ICBMs are being integrated in SS-20 launcher regiments of the Strategic Rocket Command. *Included* in the above figures are about one dozen U.S. Pershing II missiles (low-yield, short-range, single-warhead) on which the KGB Directorate for Disinformation (Service A) has focused so much world-wide propaganda. The Pershing II has about one-fifth the range, one-third the number of warheads, and roughly one-thirtieth the explosive power of the SS-20 to which it is often erroneously equated even by U.S. defense "experts." For every tactical nuclear warhead the U.S. has withdrawn, the Soviets have deployed two new ones. Numerically, the U.S. will have withdrawn *five* warheads for every Pershing II and U.S. GLCM deployed so that, on completion of the Pershing and GLCM deployments, total U.S. warheads in Europe will soon be at the lowest level in twenty years.

BOX SCORE NUMBER FIVE

CHEMICAL AND BIOLOGICAL FORCES

United States		Soviet Union
	Modern Chemical Weapon Production Facilities	
Zero		14
	Biological Weapon Production Facilities	
Zero		8
	Modern Chemical Weapons (shells, rockets, and bombs)	
Zero		700,000 tons*
	Biological Weapons	
Zero		tonnage unknown
	Estimated ICBMs for Global Chemical or Biological Weapons Delivery (SS-11 Mod 4)	
Zero		150**

Note: The United States is abiding by the 1925 Chemical Warfare Protocol and the 1972 Biological Warfare Convention and has no biological weapons or production/test facilities. In contravention of these international commitments, the Soviet Union has stockpiled biological weapons, initiated use of chemical and biological toxin weapons in combat, and conducted extensive research on and development of biological weapons (including military exploitation of genetic engineering). The Soviet advantage in offensive chemical weapons is staggering. Even in defensive terms (in which the Soviets do not often think), the Soviet advantage in decontamination equipment exceeds 25 to 1. In response to this threat, the United States has one unusable and obsolete chemical weapon production facility which ceased operation in the late 1960's. The eight Soviet biological weapons production facilities are at Sverdlovsk, Zagorsk, Omutninsk, Aksu, Pokrov, Berdsk, Penza, and Kurgan. A biological weapon storage facility is in the town of Malta. These activities are under the control of the secret 7th Main Directorate of the Soviet Ministry of Defense.

*Approximate. Stockpiled tonnage could be substantially higher.

**Highly approximate. Precise data cannot be provided.

BOX SCORE NUMBER SIX

CONVENTIONAL FORCES
(Active Components)

United States		Soviet Union
	Ground Combat Divisions	
16*		195
	Battle Force Ships	
524**		2,249
	Merchant Marine Ships	
12		1,800
	Attack Aircraft	
2,606		6,750
	Tanks	
4,960		51,900
	Armored Personnel Carriers	
7,090		63,390
	Artillery Tubes	
1,350		46,300

Note: Although Red Army Divisions (some of which are not at full strength) are smaller in troop number than U.S. Divisions, at full strength their firepower and mobility equals or exceeds that of the larger U.S. unit. Moreover, *not included* above are 250,000 troops in KGB State Security Divisions which are equipped with tanks, armored personnel carriers, and artillery and fight as conventional combat units much as did comparable Nazi SS Divisions during World War II. Also *not included* are 30 MVD Combat Divisions which perform internal security missions. The KGB troops have an equivalent strength of about 20 Soviet Army Divisions for a total (*excluding* MVD) ground combatant force of roughly 215 maneuver divisions which give a combat ratio of about 14 Soviet Divisions against one U.S. Division—not good odds. This ratio will not be materially affected by the creation of two new U.S. light divisions since the new divisions arise not from an increase in troop strength but only from an internal reorganization of the present U.S. force. The above comparison does not include non-U.S. NATO forces or non-Soviet Warsaw Pact forces which roughly balance each other and are of varying degrees of reliability and effectiveness. For similar reasons and because of the highly limited time in which any future major conventional conflict would likely be decided, active forces only are compared. Because of their specialized missions, U.S. Marine Corps and Soviet Naval Infantry are not included.

*The Cuban Army has 25 active Soviet-model combat divisions with units deployed in Central America and Africa. The Cuban *militia* is building to a level *in excess* of the combined unit strength of the entire Army, National Guard and U.S. Army Reserve.

**The degree of inferiority of the United States Navy is reduced by greater professional competence, by superior operational experience and naval tradition, and by 13 large-deck aircraft carriers. The Soviet Navy has only eight small-deck *Moskva, Kirov,* and *Kiev* class aircraft carriers but is constructing and planning at least eight large-deck nuclear-powered supercarriers as well as additional small-deck ships. The first Soviet supercarrier, *The Kremlin,* will displace 75,000 tons and will be approximately equal in size and capabilities to the very largest American carriers.

BOX SCORE NUMBER SEVEN

SPACE FORCES/STRATEGIC WEAPONS TESTING

United States		Soviet Union
	Military Space Mission Launch Sites	
25		150
	Satellite Launches Per Year	
20		100
	Payload Weight in Orbit Per Year	
30 tons		330 tons
	Ratio of Reconnaissance Satellite Launches	
1		5
	Ratio of Nuclear-Warhead Test Explosions	
1		4
	Nuclear-Warhead Test Explosions Over 150 Kilotons (per year)	
Zero		4
	Strategic Intercontinental Missile (ICBM) Tests (per year)	
5		120

Note: Anti-satellite space systems (the U.S. has none operational) are covered in Box Score Number Three. The information provided above is based necessarily on public and open official sources and accurately approximates precise data. The Soviets have developed a space-boost rocket reportedly capable of launching 150 tons into orbit in one lift. This capability could allow the Soviets, before the end of 1985, to launch an extremely large manned space station capable of housing a large number of personnel who will be in position to carry out military operations in space. The USSR has also conducted four flight tests of fighter spaceplanes which when operational will be manned by Soviet fighter pilots for direct ascent military missions in outerspace.

BOX SCORE NUMBER EIGHT

STRUCTURAL MILITARY SPENDING

United States	Soviet Union
Percentage of GNP	
5%	over 20%
Percentage of all Government Spending	
17.5%	up to 60%
Percentage of Military Spending Devoted to Development and Acquisition of Weapons and Equipment	
38%	70%
Percentage of Military Spending Devoted to Development and Acquisition of Strategic Weapons*	
5.6%	30%
Percentage of Military Spending Devoted to Personnel Costs	
44%	10%
Overall Ratio of Soviet Versus U.S. Military Spending *annually***	
1	2.5

Note: The Soviet Union spends annually at least $40 billion more than the United States on strategic nuclear systems. Defense spending under President Reagan, because of Congressional actions, is substantially *below* levels recommended by President Carter ($38 billion less) and *one-half* the percentage of Federal spending allocated by President Kennedy under whose leadership almost *fifty percent* of the Federal budget was devoted to National Defense. Sources are the Department of Defense, the Defense Intelligence Agency, and hearing records of the Subcommittee on General Procurement of the Senate Committee on Armed Services.

*The U.S. has cancelled appropriated funding for the present fiscal year to procure nuclear weapon systems for current deployment, having already cancelled further procurement of the only two systems in deployment, the Trident I and the ALCM-B. Congress (except for funds appropriated in prior years) has in fact for fiscal year 1985 frozen all U.S. strategic deployments as if a nuclear freeze were in effect.

**This estimate is based on the proportional defense burden on the respective Soviet and American Gross National Products and on the relative size of each GNP; as such it is an approximation only but is quite accurate in terms of order of magnitude. Moreover, the disparity evidenced by this rough ratio is greatly magnified by its cumulative effects over succeeding annual cycles.

BOX SCORE NUMBER NINE

SOVIET vs. CARTER vs. REAGAN
COMPARATIVE MILITARY SPENDING
(Billions of U.S. Dollars)

	1982	1983	1984	1985	1986	Total
SOVIET	360	378	418	460	480	2,096
CARTER	184	210	238	268	300	1,200
REAGAN	185	210	227	254	286*	1,162
REAGAN vs CARTER	+1	0	−11	−14	−14*	−38
U.S. vs USSR	−175	−168	−191	−206	−194*	−934

Note: The above figures are in billions of comparable U.S. dollars using, in the case of the Soviet data, Joint Chiefs of Staff (JCS) conversion techniques for converting current year rubles to current year GNP dollars. These figures represent actual defense spending (outlays) which is the best measure of Defense budgeting priorities by fiscal year. Sources are the U.S. Department of Defense, the JCS, and the Defense Intelligence Agency; however the Soviet data is approximate only. The Soviet spending data is also at variance with estimates derived from current CIA analysis which "bean counts" Soviet systems and then attempts to price each system in rubles. The CIA methodology is of doubtful validity as evidenced by the CIA decision in 1977 *to double its own estimates* on the basis of other evidence. Regrettably the flawed methodology was retained and therefore further CIA revisions are inevitable. President Reagan's defense spending is currently well *below* levels recommended by President Carter and will likely be much further reduced by Congressional action. Reagan actual spending (budget function 050) is at least 156 billion *below* the Reagan March 1981 five (5) year defense plan and (using the methodology underlying the data) approaching one trillion *below* Soviet military spending for the same five year time period. In fact, the actual disparity between U.S. and Soviet military spending could be much greater than shown above. Every penny of the Reagan defense buildup announced in March, 1981, has been *deleted* plus an *additional* cut of $38 billion.

*As of early 1985. Congressional Budget Office estimates for U.S. Military spending for FY 1986 are already substantially lower than the President's budget request shown above.

GENERAL ANALYSIS

The Dynamics of Arms

"By 1985, we will be able to extend our will wherever we wish."

Leonid Brezhnev,
in 1973.

"History will not give us a second chance."

Caspar Weinberger,
in 1985.

The overview force structures, presented in "box score" format, represent what strategic planners call a *static* analysis of the strategic potential of the United States and the Soviet Union. The authors believe that accurate and comprehensive static analysis, as shown, yields the most easily understandable summary information of current forces, but we also agree that a full assessment of relative military potential must take account of how static forces, measured in peacetime, could be actually employed in wartime. That assessment of potential actual use is termed *dynamic* analysis because it values the worth of forces not simply numerically but as potentially employed.

Unfortunately for America, a dynamic analysis of the relative Soviet threat is even less comforting than the implications to be drawn from the awesome static imbalances outlined in the box scores.

Moreover, a net general assessment of relative power is seen to be even worse from an American perspective in part because dynamic analysis, in addition to the practical use of weapons systems, also takes account of the potential *interaction* of military forces at different levels of force employment.* Obviously, in that regard, clear superiority in a higher level of force will dominate and control an opponent's equality or even superiority at a lower level.

---

*Dynamic analysis thus recognizes that forces are not merely cumulative and that a fully accurate assessment is often achieved *not* through the arithmetic of X plus Y but rather through that of X *times* Y.

Strategic planners call this latter concept "escalation dominance," meaning that superiority at the highest level will control lower levels of force and that superiority in each succeeding lower level will control force levels of even lesser degree. Obviously, dominance at a higher level coupled with dominance at a lower level gives control both directly *and* through escalation potential.

During World War II, Nazi Germany possessed large stockpiles of highly lethal chemical weapons. Yet Hitler, who was capable of any barbarism, refused to order their use. The reason is now clear. Hitler, himself badly gassed in World War I, feared American and British chemical weapons far more than he valued his own.

Yet, had *Hitler* developed the atomic bomb before his defeat and *before* its development in the United States, he almost certainly would have used not only the atomic bomb but his chemical weapons as well, because superiority at the highest level would have conferred freedom of action—freedom to act terribly—at all lower levels. Without an American atomic bomb, our matching, retaliatory use of chemical weapons would have been forestalled because of fear that the Nazi would exact even greater nuclear retribution.

Fortunately for the Allies, Hitler never attained "escalation dominance," the War in Europe did not escalate, and the Allies achieved victory through conventional warfare. In the Pacific, the United States (balanced with Japan in chemical weapons) achieved *and used* "escalation dominance" by attacking Japan with *atomic* weapons. That action ended further Japanese resistance potential at the chemical and even conventional level. In short, the top of the force pyramid governed the broader bases, and history teaches that escalation dominance is more than theory.

Today, the Soviet Union has attained military superiority at *every* force level. Russia dominates the pyramid from top to bottom. That central fact is evident in even the most casual study of the "box scores" earlier reviewed. But what precisely do these static imbalances mean in dynamic terms? What do they mean in terms of the potential use of power and its effect on policy?

Soviet Strategic Dominance

At the top of the power pyramid, the USSR now has an effective overall static advantage of about *six to one* over the United States in strategic nuclear offensive and anti-nuclear defensive forces. This imbalance suggests in dynamic terms that the Soviet Union now has the "first strike" potential so long feared by American strategists. But worse still, the apparent Soviet first strike potential (in which ICBM countersilo warheads predominate) grows ever more ominous each year, and its utility to the Communists for nuclear blackmail and intimidation becomes ever more obvious. No one today could reasonably be accused of overstating the facts by insisting that the growing Soviet first strike capability does indeed throw a darkening shadow over the entire world.

In a general sense, therefore, the static imbalances in strategic nuclear and anti-nuclear strategic defensive forces more than support the dynamic analysis leading to recent assessments from senior Department of Defense officials that the Soviet Union is *10 years* ahead of the United States in strategic offensive capabilities and is also 10 years ahead of America in strategic *defensive* anti-ballistic missile, anti-air, and civil population protection capabilities.

These "top of the pyramid" nuclear offensive and anti-nuclear defensive Soviet advantages now plainly possessed by our opponent should not be surprising. We have had ample warning.

As long ago as 1969, a senior Soviet military leader explained the growth of Soviet military forces and military industry when he made the following statement in a classified Soviet military journal*:

"Strengthening of its defenses is now the *foremost* political function of the Soviet state . . . Never before has the internal life of the country been subordinated to a *war* so deeply and thoroughly as at the present."

Since 1973, the Soviets have spent far in excess of $460 billion on *procurement* of military weapons alone. The USSR has dedicated a larger share of its natural and industrial resources, year after year, to the production of military weapons *than any other country has ever done in peacetime.* The ongoing

*Major General Korniyenko, in *Military Thought.*

expansion and modernization of the Soviet industrial base, as well as sustained high levels of activity in weapons research and development, indicate that production of advanced military equipment and materiel will not only continue, but will probably *increase* in the future.

Since 1970, Soviets have increased their military production floorspace by about a third. Since 1970, the major Soviet weapons plants have nearly doubled in size and there has been continuous expansion and modernization of key missile producing facilities. And notwithstanding the already incredibly high levels of present production, the USSR is still increasing output in virtually every category of military hardware.

The Soviets have 135 major military industrial plants in operation. These facilities produce more than 150 different types of weapons and vast guantities of ammunitions. And according to a report of the Department of Defense issued in 1984:

"Since 1970, the Soviets have developed more than 20 new types of [military] aircraft, 10 new types of ballistic missiles, 25 new types of aerodynamic missiles, over 50 new classes of naval ships, one third of which have been submarines, and at least 50 new ground force weapons."

Thus, past proven performance and evident current trends indicate that the Soviet military buildup will continue relentlessly and indefinitely, and is open-ended in scope. In every aspect, the present determination of the Soviet Union to produce mass quantities of major weapons systems in a "peacetime" environment is unmatched by any nation in the world today or in history. No country has ever equaled the proven will and capacity now demonstrated by the Soviets to build so much for war in time of "peace."

Worse still, because Soviet planners understand the doctrine of escalation dominance, the Soviet effort has placed first production priority at the apex of the strategic pyramid: in strategic nuclear forces and strategic defenses against U.S. nuclear forces.

These Soviet offensive and defensive advantages gravely threaten—have already almost eliminated—the effectiveness of our retaliatory deterrent, which guarded against Soviet escalation dominance and preserved the world peace for 40 years.

In short, if the Soviets can now threaten a devastating first strike while making clear they can parry a great part of any remaining U.S. retaliatory response, deterrence of nuclear war is gravely weakened. Peace could be in jeopardy, and the U.S. could be not only vulnerable to a Soviet first strike, but more importantly, *because of its vulnerability* America could be increasingly subject to Soviet coercion and intimidation through the power implicit in an overwhelming nuclear advantage.

The developing situation is not at all unlike the great flux of history which threatened Nazi dominance over the democracies in the mid-1930's. With American politicians clamoring to kiss the ring of Mr. Gromyko lest they incur any hint of Soviet disfavor, our times are not at all unlike those described by Winston Churchill in July, 1936:

> "The months slip by rapidly, if we delay too long in repairing our defenses, *we may be forbidden by superior power to complete the process.* I say there is a state of emergency. We are in danger as we have never been in danger before."

With no doubt less eloquence but with no less force, many dedicated government servants are today attempting to warn of far worse dangers in Soviet strategic nuclear dominance.

For example, Assistant Secretary of Defense Richard Perle recently told Congress that there has been almost a 75% increase in Soviet nuclear warheads aimed at the United States just since the SALT II Treaty was signed in 1979. During that period, the Soviets have deployed at least 3,850 new strategic nuclear warheads, and that figure does not count their missile refire capability and their capacity for further salvoes.

As Secretary of Defense Weinberger stated on December 20, 1984:

> "Improvements and additions to the Soviet Missile force continue at a frightening pace, even though we have added SALT II restraints on top of SALT I agreements. The Soviet Union has built *more* of the big nuclear warheads capable of destroying U.S. missiles in their concrete silos than we initially predicted they would build, even *without* any SALT agreement. *We now confront precisely the situation that the SALT process was intended to prevent.*"

31

These staggering new missile deployments mean that the Soviets are close to *doubling* (and may have already doubled) the number of nuclear warheads aimed at America since former President Carter signed SALT II in order to "limit" nuclear arms.

Few Americans understand that fact . . . much less its implications. We will examine those implications now, and hopefully dispel the tragically widespread error that nuclear force levels and anti-nuclear defenses do not matter since "there are already enough nuclear bombs to destroy the world."

First, we must remember that in the past, American deterrence of nuclear attack depended on a triad of nuclear forces created initially for defensive purposes to assure escalation dominance at the highest level. This triad stood on three legs: 1) intercontinental ballistic missiles (ICBMs); 2) intercontinental bombers; and 3) submarine launched ballistic missiles (SLBMs). But today, all three legs of the U.S. triad are vulnerable, or will be soon, to a Soviet first strike:

- At this moment, all U.S. ICBMs can be overwhelmed by the enormous Soviet advantage in accurate anti-silo ICBM warheads. 7,000 Soviet anti-silo warheads are more than sufficient for *all* 1000 U.S. silos. The Defense Intelligence Agency estimates that *with just two Soviet warheads targeted per U.S. ICBM silo* more than 90% would be destroyed leaving more than 5000 Soviet warheads (of which some would be on the way) to finish off the surviving 100 U.S. silos housing any remaining U.S. missiles. (See Box Score Number 1.)

- Nearly all U.S. strategic bombers are also vulnerable (and *all* soon will be) due to the continuing Soviet advances in ICBM, SLBM, cruise missile, and air defense capabilities. (See particularly Box Score Number 3 dealing with strategic defenses.) Already about 75% of our bombers are vulnerable on the ground, and the initially survivable 25% on ground alert face ever diminishing prospects of penetrating the already astonishingly formidable and constantly improving Soviet air defenses.

  The U.S. bomber force is also totally obsolete. The aircraft are older than the average age of the crew members flying them. (One pilot was heard to say, "We used to worry about getting back; now we just worry about getting there.") Moreover, bomber readiness and availability for strategic missions has been even further reduced by the dedication of some B-52s to naval interdiction and conventional bombing missions. And, despite the fine sounding rhetoric and glossy photographs, *no* B-1B bombers are yet operational. When the first ones are, in late 1986, their numbers will be few and they will face essentially the same problems as the B-52s.

- Since most of our land-based missiles and bombers would perish in the first salvo, *we are now and will continue throughout the 1980s to be unduly reliant on the third leg of our Triad, the sea-based SLBM force*, for most of our nuclear deterrence. But many SLBMs are reportedly dedicated to targets outside the USSR and therefore probably ought not even be reckoned in the top-line strategic intercontinental force level at all. Moreover, the number of our deployable submarines, SLBMs, SLBM warheads, and SLBM megatonnage has been drastically reduced by the premature and irreversable retirement of ten Polaris SLBM submarines before they could be replaced by the newer Trident boats.

Furthermore, the Extremely Low Frequency (ELF) submarine communications system will not be operational until 1986, thereby dangerously extending the period during which our missile submarines will be especially vulnerable to detection and destruction since they must patrol close to the surface in order to communicate via normal radio. Meanwhile, the USSR has been reported to have developed and placed in orbit a prototype space-based Synthetic Aperture Radar to conduct wide ocean search for *submerged* U.S. submarines. If the Soviets can thus make the oceans transparent through high technology, then all U.S. submarines could be attacked underwater by a variety of means including barrage fire of undersea exploding nuclear warheads from, for example, the Soviet SS-20 ballistic missile.

Finally, *less than 50% (about 15 subs) of our much reduced submarine force of only 35 SLBM submarines is on patrol at any one time.* And even more alarming is the fact that reportedly only *three patrolling subs* carrying a total of *48 SLBMs* may be in communication with the National Command Authority at any one time, and hence *at this very moment* only this very small force may be *actually capable* of retaliation to a nuclear strike. And on top of this, all of our strategic command and control systems are themselves vulnerable to nuclear strike so that the Soviets could plausibly believe that even these three submarines might never receive the order to launch.

In sum, two and a half legs of the U.S. Triad are now vulnerable, and the remaining half-leg of the Triad (strategic submarines on patrol) may itself also be vulnerable already . . . or soon will be. Thus, at the top of the pyramid of forces *the vulnerability of our strategic forces is at an all time high.**

Accordingly, the degree of survivability of our vital three SLBM submarines in communication with the National Command Authority (and of that communication link itself) remains one of the most significant unknown factors in U.S. national security calculations. And there can be little solace found in our knowledge that the Soviets are spending over three times more than the U.S. an Anti-Submarine Warfare (ASW) and that Russia has almost *three times* as many attack (ASW) submarines as the U.S. (See Box Score Number 3.)

As a Director of U.S. Naval Intelligence has noted, the Soviets' "extensive ASW Research and Development effort . . . is the area in which we could be expected to know *the least,* because it does not have the manifestations in the open seas that their weapons and platforms do." Nevertheless, as indicated in Box Score Number 3, *we now have public reports that the Soviets are currently testing, in space and aboard aircraft prototypes of high-technology systems designed to locate U.S. Submarines underwater in broad ocean areas.* And even more significant, there are reports that the Soviets have already deployed at least two operational space-based Anti-Submarine Warfare detection systems.**

---

*A number of reasonable Americans engaged in the business of analyzing nuclear forces believe that only a handful of surviving nuclear warheads should be sufficient to deter Soviet attack. This line of thought is called the doctrine of "minimum deterrence." Unfortunately, the issue is not what the proponents of this doctrine believe but rather whether the Soviets also believe in it, and the evidence is overwhelming that they do not. Why else, for example, would the Soviets be willing virtually to wreck their economy in order to build nuclear weapons and anti-nuclear defenses if they felt that only a handful of surviving American weapons could be a complete deterrent and prevent the use of the Soviet advantage either in negotiation or in war?

**A Defense Intelligence Agency report has been quoted as saying that the Soviet space-based ASW radar effort "is a matter of concern because it demonstrates that the Soviets are determined to destroy all three legs of the U.S. deterrent Triad if they possibly can find the means to do so."

Because the 48 or so SLBMs on board the three ballistic missile submarines in communication with the National Command Authority may, in fact, constitute the actual U.S. strategic deterrent at any one time, this limited number of missiles could, therefore, suddenly become vulnerable to an unanticipated Soviet breakthrough in ASW, about which "we could be expected to know the least." Moreover, even if these 48 SLBMs, or even additional U.S. SLBMs, could be ordered to launch, the relatively slow-flying SLBMs and non-maneuvering SLBM warheads would have to penetrate the Moscow antimissile defense and the developing nationwide Soviet ABM defense which deploys the SA-12 and other anti-SLBM rockets. And that retaliatory U.S. launch, even if successfully ordered *and executed*, would be suicidal for the United States if it *triggered withheld Soviet second, third, and fourth strikes against a defenseless America.* What practical value would there be, indeed, in a relatively ineffectual retaliation by a limited number of American submarines which would only bring unmitigated further destruction to our own homeland?

The key point is this: compounding the danger of Soviet strategic offensive superiority (see Box Score Number 1) is the fact that the Soviets possess a balanced array of highly capable strategic defenses and reserve forces. (See Box Score Numbers 2 and 3.) As a result of U.S. unilateral "restraint"* and of Congressional cuts, the U.S. now has no ABM system, no effective strategic defenses of any type, and no strategic reserves whatsoever.

On the other hand, the Soviets, no doubt appropriately moved by American "restraint" and by our Congress, have already deployed the most extensive anti-ballistic missile (ABM), air defense missile and fighter-interceptor systems ever built. Moreover, the Soviet ABM and air defense systems are being rapidly modernized and expanded. Their air defense missiles and radars also have a significant ABM capability.

---

*The word "restraint" is the favored euphemism at the Department of State for American inaction or appeasement regarding whatever Soviet challenge. "Restraint" is seen often in official correspondence where it is most frequently used to explain away gross U.S. defense deficiencies in terms of *mollifying* Russia in the naive but apparently eternal hope of *modifying* Soviet aggressiveness. It is one of three magic words in Washington, the other two being "concerns" and "meaningful" as in "We share your *concerns* that we have a *meaningful* dialogue on a basis of mutual *restraint,*" i.e., "Let's talk." (For a Department of State drafted textual example, please see Appendix III.)

But of even greater significance, the Soviets have already begun (almost openly and contemptuously) to "break out" of the SALT I ABM Treaty and are in the process of making fully operational a rapidly deployable, *nationwide defense against U.S. ballistic missiles*. Remember also that the Soviets have a huge and still expanding civil defense system which promises to limit significantly casualties and damage in nuclear war. They also have the world's only operational Anti-Satellite (ASAT) systems. Additionally, the Soviet advantages and emphasis on strategic ASW here noted may be the final capability needed by Russia *to checkmate the entire U.S. deterrent*. Finally, the Soviets are expediting development of advanced charged particle beam and laser weapons technology, and they may well achieve a revolutionary anti-ballistic missile (ABM) and space defense capability based on weapons using new physical principles long before the United States.*

In that connection, the Soviets are now estimated to be working on a high technology, space-based ABM that could be launched as early as 1986. If they bring this off, then again, whatever limited U.S. deterrence remained could be finally eliminated and America prohibited from deploying any similar defensive system as a result of that quantum leap in Soviet strategic power.

In fact, on October 18, 1984, in a 36 page analysis released to the public, the Defense Intelligence Agency warned that Soviet intentions were precisely "to acquire superiority in outer space" and at the same time to use space systems and space weapons to support Soviet combat units on earth. The DIA analysis also confirmed that *a major purpose* of those efforts is "*to deny* the use of outer space to [the United States]" and that "the military nature of much of the USSR's space capabilities is *overwhelmingly offensive* in character, since that is the essence of their military doctrine." The DIA report concluded that the Soviets have tested two laser-beam weapons with sufficient power to down satellites, and it supported a similar CIA assessment that "the Soviets [will] begin to place in orbit . . . systems capable of effectively attacking . . . ground, sea, and air targets *from space*."

---

*The Soviets are already testing anti-satellite, high-energy gas dynamic and iodine lasers at the Saryshagan test site. U.S. analysts believe that deployment of a ground-based laser weapon system at locations throughout the USSR is in the offing. *Pravda,* in the fall of 1984, announced that the Soviet Union would deploy a high-energy laser in space in 1985.

These were very grave tidings: but they were entirely lost on the American public and on an ever silent news media. So, to reiterate: a Soviet technological breakthrough in space warfare is not science fiction. It is very nearly history. When it does come, it could end the prospect of deploying any related U.S. space technology and *will end* any remaining semblance of U.S. nuclear deterrent.

In 1981 Senate testimony acknowledging the then already substantial Soviet first-strike capability and growing nuclear superiority (as well presumably as Soviet advances in space weaponry), Secretary of Defense Caspar Weinberger stated that the "window of vulnerability will be at its widest in the period of 1985-1986." Thus, as bad as the strategic disadvantages of the U.S. are now, in terms of almost any rational forecast, they will get worse. In that regard, one consideration alone should be sufficient to make the point: between now and 1990, the USSR will add, according to our best intelligence projections, at least 10,000 additional new ICBM warheads to an existing force of roughly 20,000. Under these conditions, Secretary Weinberger's warning that "history will not give us a second chance" is valuable but seriously understated.

On November 16, 1934, Winston Churchill reminded the House of Commons:

"Peace must be founded on preponderance."

Churchill called for a 4 to 1 superiority over totalitarian armed strength.

But today, in early 1985, at the highest level of force dominance, it is the Soviet Union which has an overall 6 to 1 static advantage over the United States and clear superiority in any dynamic analysis of the potential use of that advantage, especially when Soviet strategic defenses and reserves are also taken into account.

In summary, the entire U.S. strategic deterrent could soon be rendered vulnerable to either a potential Soviet first strike or to completed Soviet defenses. *International recognition of this almost complete U.S. vulnerability would be the end of deterrence and would end American protection of liberty* because American freedom of action at other force levels, down even to the modest pressure of diplomacy and trade, would be effectively throttled by the entrenchment of the Soviet Union on the commanding heights of world power—at the highest level of strategic force—the capability of destroying or negating American nuclear forces while retaining unused massive residual nuclear firepower.

But Soviet dominance does not end at the top of the pyramid. It continues down to its base.

Tactical Nuclear Forces

Below the level of strategic nuclear weapons, the Soviet Union is so armed as to be able also to dominate escalation at the tactical nuclear level, that is, at the level of potential employment of less powerful, shorter range nuclear weapons in a continental or local rather than global theater of war.

A quick reference to Box Score Number 4 shows the current static advantage in tactical nuclear forces favoring Russia. That already significant advantage is further compounded by the probability that some *strategic* SS-20 warheads are in fact programmed by the Soviets for regional use. And so, here again, the Soviet first strike potential would suffice to eliminate U.S. tactical nuclear weapons which cannot in any event be used themselves in a first strike *because of the awesome threat posed by Soviet dominance at the strategic level.*

Moreover, unlike the United States, the Soviet Union has *not* shown "restraint" in developing anti-tactical nuclear missile (ATM) systems and has openly acknowledged the ability of several types of ATM weapons (for example, the SA-12) to destroy U.S. tactical missiles in flight. Additionally, Soviet fighters (for example the MIG-23M, MIG-25M, MIG-29, MIG-31, and SU-27) have a look-down, shoot-down capability which allows them to destroy slow flying U.S. cruise missiles.* The net result is that any residual American tactical nuclear forces surviving a Soviet first strike would be unlikely to penetrate Soviet ATM defenses.

In summary, because of pronounced Soviet strategic nuclear preponderance, the United States *cannot* risk using tactical nuclear weapons first, the USSR *can* risk using tactical nuclear weapons first, and the Soviets *can* defend against any residual or retaliatory U.S. tactical nuclear counterattack. Russia, in other words, by tactical preponderance and defenses (and by strategic superiority) dominates and would decide and control escalation to tactical nuclear forces.

*The Soviets are also likely to provide this capability to the high-technology MIG-2000 now in research and development.

Chemical and Biological Forces

The Soviet advantage in this catagory is so large as to be incalculable, but the Soviet Union enjoys *at least* a 1,000 to 1 advantage in deliverable modern chemical munitions. The Soviet Union enjoys an unknown advantage in biological weapons. (See Box Score Number 5.)

The United States does not possess biological weapons and its chemical weapons are obsolete, leaking, and almost as dangerous to our own forces as to the Soviets. Yet, Congress and apologists for the Soviets in Congress and on Congressional staffs continue to delay the development and production of modern, safe-to-handle U.S. binary chemical weapons.

The Soviet Union also has roughly a 35 to 1 advantage over the United States in *defending* against chemical and biological attack. Soviet troops routinely train in a chemical environment (at times with lethal agents) to improve their defenses and have used chemical and biological weapons in combat operations.* American troops rarely train in a chemical environment and have in any event only small quantities of *effective* defensive equipment.

In the past, as the American chemical weapon stockpile became of less and less value through obsolescence, American *defense* against chemical and biological weapons was increasingly predicated on the deterrence of potential American escalation to use of tactical nuclear weapons in retaliation for Soviet chemical or biological attack. That threat of nuclear escalation is no longer believable (or "credible" to use the strategists' phrase) because the USSR now dominates at both the tactical *and strategic* nuclear level. Accordingly, at the chemical/biological level the Soviet Union with superior chemical forces and a monopoly in biological forces dominates yet again as our analysis proceeds down the force pyramid.

And our next result is even less reassuring.

---

*The USSR operates over 200 separate chemical/biological warfare training sites, maintains 30,000 military vehicles dedicated to chemical/biological decontamination and detection, and has a wartime force of over 160,000 men exclusively designated for chemical/biological/radiological defense. The Soviets or their clients have used chemical and biological weapons in Laos, Cambodia, and Afghanistan and have equipped Cuba with a huge chemical and biological weapons storage facility. They are currently also providing chemical warfare training and equipment to Nicaragua.

Conventional Forces

The USSR (see Box Score Number 6) maintains a 14 to 1 static advantage in combat divisions coupled with overwhelming advantages in artillery, armor, airborne troops, ground attack and fighter aircraft, and—to a degree—strategic mobility. Soviet conventional naval forces also outnumber American forces but the Soviet advantage here is perhaps less obvious than in ground and air forces. As a result, in terms of dynamic application of Soviet conventional forces, the geographic area of potential operations becomes a significant factor. Nonetheless, the Soviet Navy with several nuclear powered supercarriers under construction is growing at a tremendous pace, and the existing degree of Soviet dominance at the conventional level remains high on a global basis. Here is why.

First, there is already ample reason to believe that Soviet conventional forces clearly dominate in Europe, in Asia, and more recently in the Middle East. As with tactical nuclear and chemical forces, in these regions a Soviet first strike with conventional forces would have a high probability for success in eliminating any defending American force. Moreover, a conventional first strike by American forces in these same geographic areas (besides being politically implausible) would be easily contained by the Soviets and would invite a devastating conventional counterattack with marked potential for Soviet escalation to higher force levels.

Perhaps for reasons of those realities, U.S. military service schools, like the Army Command and General Staff College, practically never admit the possibility of, much less advocate, an unlimited conventional *American* counterattack and speak instead solely in terms of defensive objectives and "restoring the borders." Yet, in the operational areas in question, the balance of conventional force so clearly favors the USSR that even the limited American objective of regaining invaded territory is of doubtful practicality.

Second, in Africa and in the Americas, Soviet superiority at the conventional level may also eventually control. Although Russia now only maintains two Soviet combat brigades in Cuba and limited Cuban proxy forces in Africa and Central America, the expanding Soviet Navy can already project substantial conventional combat power even in the Gulf of Mexico and Caribbean Sea. Additionally, Soviet construction of several large-deck nuclear aircraft carriers at the Nikolayev

Shipyard on the Black Sea suggests a planned power-projection force of at least eight carrier battle groups. These new supercarriers (the first is near completion) will further drive the conventional balance toward greater Soviet dominance even in the Americas.

Third, whereas twenty years ago the Soviets could pose no serious threat to world sea lanes on which American global defense and commerce depend, the Soviet Navy may now be capable of closing several maritime choke points with superior conventional force.

With Soviet supremacy at higher force levels, what response could the United States risk if, for example, the Soviets on some pretext chose to close the Dardenelles or even Gibraltar or the Straits of Hormuz? Having seen American paralysis during the hostage crisis just in dealing with *Iran*, we can, not unfairly, assume the worst and ask further what results would American *inaction* bring for our friends and allies in Israel and Japan to whom these sea lanes are even more critical than to us? Unlike a decade past (when America had a Navy with one thousand ships and there was not a Soviet nuclear submarine base in Cuba), these possibilities can no longer be ignored.

Finally, even if the United States can still achieve conventional dominance (including naval dominance) in a particular area and time, for example in Central America or on and around Caribbean Islands like Grenada, if the Soviets choose to act or threaten action elsewhere, our remaining regional abilities can be effectively negated through the gigantic edge the Soviets maintain in Europe and the Middle East. With Soviet combat forces already stationed in Syria and with West Berlin surrounded by Russian tanks, we can easily speculate on the possible Soviet response to any truly serious *direct* effort by the United States to turn back Communism in Nicaragua or El Salvador, or even in Guatamala or Honduras.

The point is this: enormous Soviet conventional dominance in Europe backed by Soviet dominance in chemical and biological forces, in tactical nuclear forces, and in strategic nuclear forces checkmates any *significant* use of conventional force by the United States *anywhere*, even if America can still achieve local dominance. Stated simply, the Soviet Union dominates *overall* at the conventional level and can control and limit any U.S. move to escalate to conventional counterattack when, for example, Soviet proxies conduct guerrilla offensives—as in El Salvador.*

Terrorism and Revolution

Moving from the conventional stage still further down the force pyramid, the strategist encounters so-called "low-intensity conflict." Here are the "wars of national liberation", the "anti-colonial insurgencies," and the state-sponsored terrorism of the PLO, the KGB, and the Cuban and Bulgarian Secret Services. Here also are the counter-insurgency and counter-revolutionary operations of U.S. Special Forces and of the anti-Communist "Contras" based in Honduras.

Here too, as evidenced by a seventy-year history of virtually unbroken success, the Soviet Union holds clear dominance. In static terms Russia has several hundred thousand KGB agents and 50 thousand Spetnaz troops conducting, organizing, and planning terrorism and insurgencies, while the United States has less than 4,500 active duty troops in Special Forces units and about an equal number of Congressional prohibitions.

At present, the Soviet Union is supporting at least seven *separate* significant insurgencies worldwide and conducts terrorism with impunity—even to include an attempt to kill the Pope—because the Soviet Union dominates this form of warfare *and* all levels of escalation above it.

And since the support of terrorism and revolution is the lowest risk *violent* means of achieving Communist objectives, it is *the preferred* force level employed by the Soviet Union . . . and Soviet dominance above at all levels of escalation permits little more in response than the obligatory handful of American counter-insurgency advisors and an eventual negotiated settlement on Soviet terms.

---

*Understanding this latter dynamic makes clear why President Reagan has as yet taken no *significant* action against Soviet-controlled Nicaragua even though the President fully recognizes that Nicaraguan Communism is a direct threat to the United States because of its potential for support of Soviet strategic air and naval power in operations in the Western Hemisphere and because of its inevitable and growing destabilizing effect on 75 million Mexicans on our southern border.

Diplomacy and International Trade

The next level down the force pyramid does not involve force at all, at least not directly, but it does involve the potential for using force successfully. This form of conflict is at the level of international negotiation and trade relations.

In the early days of the Roman Empire (*circa* 390 B.C.), the barbarian conqueror Brennus arrived with his army at the outskirts of the city of Rome but did not enter. Instead he suggested the negotiation of some appropriate amount of "foreign aid" for his cause.

The Roman leaders brought gold and weighed it out on a balance scale as ransom for the city. When they had paid all they *thought* they could and had balanced the barbarian's lead weights with Roman gold, the barbarian commander, exclaiming "woe to the conquered," threw his sword into the scale on the side with the lead, and the city fathers, understanding the message, sought even more gold to balance out the invader's sword as well.

Today, Western diplomacy, grounded in the principles of "restraint," has, over several decades, increasingly resembled the diplomacy of those civic men of ancient Rome. Our diplomats prefer to heap on gold when the Russians throw on swords.

Highly concessional credits for grain purchases, massive Western interbank deposits at no interest in Soviet banks, a one-half billion dollar U.S. Government loan bail-out for Communist Poland, the recent rescheduling of the $3.5 billion Cuban Communist debt to Western governments and banks, the return of Communist Czechoslovakian gold reserves while Czechoslovakia refuses to repay American citizens, technology transfers including even the means for ensuring accurate guidance of Soviet nuclear warheads, and a fawning non-response to the Soviet murder of an anti-Soviet Congressman and 268 other innocent men, women, and children: these tell the tale of Soviet control of the force pyramid and how that dominance induces cowardice in American foreign policy and in international commerce.

But supine behavior induced by Soviet power does not end at American shores.

Internal Politics and Domestic Policy

At the lowest level of the pyramid of forces is the effect of international conflict in the domestic politics and the moral health of the nation. And yes, here too the Soviet Union dominates this most fundamental form of struggle.

Whereas Russia is a closed society upon which the United States has virtually no capacity for effecting any internal alteration, America is open, holds free elections, and allows a free press to disseminate truth and falsehood . . . with sanctions of disapproval applied more often to the true than to the false. By the very nature of our freedoms, Soviet dominance in manipulating domestic policy in the West is almost an inevitability. But without Soviet dominance at other levels of power, the Soviet program of interference with the internal policies of the United States could be more effectively curtailed. At the moment, many American leaders feel they must tolerate Soviet influences in America because more open resistance might cause the Soviets to escalate to terrorism* . . . to which level the USSR can move at will through proxies very ready to hand . . . or to bring about the leader's electoral defeat by generating and reinforcing public fear of the dangers of anti-Soviet attitudes and actions.

Thus, America is being brought gradually under increased Soviet influence. Thus, Americans are conditioned to see nothing abnormal in both candidates for the American Presidency meeting with the Soviet Foreign Minister, unabashedly seeking his blessing and good offices at the height of a national political campaign. Thus, Congress looks over its shoulder at Soviet might on every vote on major military programs lest it give offense to the Kremlin. Thus, America sanctions brutal life-denying social policies, accepts attacks on the family and

*To understand the reality of this threat, one need only contemplate the presently on-going construction of anti-terrorist barriers around the Pentagon and even the White House complex itself.

religion, and subtly teaches its youth a form of state-sponsored secular humanism much akin to the theory of man and athiest orthodoxy on which Marxism is founded.*

And, the American governmental response to this broad-based Soviet-inspired assault on our very fiber as a people has been little more than the timid and tepid broadcasts of the Voice of America which is perpetually mindful of the scope of Soviet power and dominance, and of the resulting need to show deference, and, yes . . . *restraint.*

Climbing the Pyramid

To end American paralysis and our lingering sickness of soul and mind, Americans must understand the tragedy of how we got in our present predicament and how best to regain ascendency and safety. That is the single not immodest but very hopeful purpose of this book.

To carry out that process, more Americans must first recognize the present danger and the follies that have led to it, and second, we must in sufficient numbers develop collectively a rational approach to recovering lost strength. The road to U.S. strategic inferiority has been long (and the road to recovery will be longer) but several milestones of our downward slide can now be recalled usefully in this introductory analysis.

Here are a few:

- Since 1977, when the Carter-Mondale Administration began, more than 710 U.S. strategic delivery vehicles and over 6,000 strategic nuclear warheads that were previously planned by the Ford Administration to be added to U.S. strategic forces by 1985 were instead unilaterally

---

*A friend from the Vietnam War who was recently in Washington, D.C., for the January, 1985, right to life demonstrations told us that he had been "proud to fight for the United States fifteen years ago" but that he now felt "no obligation whatsoever to a society that condones and encourages the premeditated murder of 5 million babies each year . . . the United States has become like a silver goblet filled to the brim with spit." We fully understand the passion of that sentiment but suspect that fostering feelings of that type, although they are justified, is one of the very goals of those who deny the moral accountability of individuals to each other and of nations to each life.

cut. They have not been restored by President Reagan. In fact, since *1962*, more than 4,000 U.S. strategic nuclear delivery vehicles carrying over 10,000 nuclear warheads have been *unilaterally deactivated* by the U.S. in order to show *restraint* in the misguided hope that Russia would follow suit. Meanwhile, the Soviets have fully deactivated almost no nuclear systems on the basis of obsolescence, have retained comparable systems to those we have destroyed, and have added countless new nuclear weapons including over 1,250 new intercontinental missile launchers and bombers carrying over 6,000 additional nuclear warheads *just since SALT negotiations began in 1969.*

- In 1975, Congress ordered dismantled the American Safeguard Anti-Ballistic Missile (ABM) system. Russia *kept* its GALOSH ABM system and developed the ABM-3, SA-5, SA-10, and SA-12 anti-missile rockets.

- In 1977, the Carter-Mondale Administration banned production of the U.S. Minuteman III ICBM, destroyed the Minuteman production facility, and cancelled and thus delayed the B-1. (The United States *still* has *no* operational B-1s.)

- A series of Administrations delayed the crucial Trident II SLBM—in order to satisfy arms control limits the Soviets were violating and to demonstrate further American *restraint*, all with the end result that this long-planned strategic missile cannot now become available *even under the most optimistic estimates* until after 1990.

- Congress in 1983-1984 stopped the U.S. Anti-Satellite program dead in its tracks (having previously delayed it) and grossly underfunded the proposed space-based American defense against Soviet ICBMs while Russia maintained *four* operational ASAT systems and proceeded with full funding for space warfare.

The foregoing items are a *few examples only*; the list of terminated and impeded American defense programs could extend almost without end.

But we must not dwell on these tragic errors of the past, grave as they have been. We must instead find a path back to the summit of the force pyramid using a practical approach.

Since it is not feasible to regain superiority at all levels at once, we must identify where our efforts are best expended and not waste energy or resources on lesser results. In that regard, since the highest level of force dominates all lower, we must first seek to restore American escalation dominance at the top.

We must, therefore, immediately reverse the precipitous decline in our strategic nuclear deterrence. We must do so by regaining superior strategic nuclear forces at levels that can control nuclear escalation and thus *prevent* nuclear war and at the same time *end* the deleterious effect of the present *Soviet* nuclear supremacy on *all other force levels*.

Also at the paramount strategic level, we must *affirmatively* protect Americans from Soviet nuclear attack by developing and building high-technology, anti-nuclear space defenses. The President's Strategic Defense Initiative (mockingly nicknamed "Star Wars" by the press) is thus of critical importance.

Simultaneously, we must never lose sight of the lasting truth that our greatest strength is our cause itself: freedom . . . and the intrepid will and individual resourcefulness derived from the still inherent capacity of Americans to act as free men.

Like Churchill, we must therefore seek to restore the spirit he called forth when explaining the tragedy overtaking the Free World in 1938:

> "The whole equilibrium has been deranged, and the terrible words have . . . been pronounced against the Western democracies: *'Thou art weighed in the balance and found wanting.'* And do not suppose that this is the end. This is only the beginning of the reckoning. This is only the first sip, the first foretaste of a bitter cup which will be proffered to us year by year unless by a supreme recovery of moral health and martial vigor, we arise again and take our stand for freedom as in the olden time."

We of the West must take that stand again today. We must reaffirm that "It is the man of faith who is ever the man of works."*

To restore the full spirit of freedom, we must accordingly regain American superiority at the *very base* of the strategic

*Captain A. T. Mahan, U.S. Navy, in his *Life of Nelson*, Vol. II, at p. 306 (Little, Brown, and Company, 1897).

pyramid . . . at the level of individual determination and action and of collective purpose . . . seeking always to be sustained and guided by the ultimate power which is at once both the foundation of liberty and the summit of life.

Fallacies About Fallout and 'Nuclear Winter'

Not included in the 'Box Scores' or dynamic analysis are the facts and figures revealing the full extent to which the Soviets have already gone in order to protect their country from the effects of a nuclear war.

These preparations are so extensive (yet virtually unknown to the American people) that there can no longer be any reason to misunderstand the reason for them. Again and again, Soviet military and political leaders have made it eminently clear in their official writings that they are seeking the ability to fight and win a nuclear war and to gain the international power advantage inherent in that capability. Unlike us, the Soviets have realistically assessed the potential effects of a nuclear exchange and have not allowed themselves to be misled by irrational fear based on inaccurate and flawed assumptions. Indeed, there is extensive evidence that the fostering of such fears in the United States and Europe has been a carefully conceived part of the Soviet plan for eventual victory.

When Franklin Roosevelt warned in 1933 that "we have nothing to fear but fear itself," he did not mean there was nothing to fear, but rather that the fearful anticipation of known or unknown dangers could not be allowed to enervate private will or debilitate public action. He intended to arouse a nation to hope. He was making a promise in the American grain: that a free nation of spirit could achieve anything it set out to, if it let its resources and resourcefulness be multiplied by its courage, not divided by its doubts.

A generation after the United States rebuilt first itself and then half the world, shattered the Third Reich and the Japanese Empire, we have seen fear itself triumph: not in some pell-mell panic, not in some disgraceful flight which might be remembered and shamefully regretted, but gradually and imperceptibly.

Gradually, very gradually, our resolve to defend ourselves has become paralyzed by "fear itself" and, specifically, by prevailing popular but incorrect assumptions about the probable characteristics of a nuclear war. Although understandable, those intense fears and their pervasive psychological effects have done much harm to the chances of lasting peace by preventing us from taking precisely those steps most critical to reducing the risks of intercontinental war.

In a sense, our fear in the presence of awesome prospects has led to irrational assessments and to the inertia that has caused those very prospects to become awesomely more possible. By burying our heads in the sand we have not only experienced the bliss of intellectual ignorance but also exposed the body to far greater and more substantial dangers. In many ways, our national paralysis of terrified illogic and the resulting actual increased exposure to risk have been the primary by-products of fundamental misunderstandings about nuclear effects, chiefly radioactive fallout.

Among many notable published contributions to these false perceptions, and to making the already horrible become totally unthinkable in any realistic manner (and thus more likely), was Neville Shute's widely-promoted novel of the late 1950's, *On The Beach.* This superb example of the propaganda of fear postulated a world gradually and entirely destroyed by radioactive fallout from a superpower nuclear war. The book was fiction in more ways than one, but its pseudoscientific, back-of-the-envelope thesis, although now known to be wrong, was, and unfortunately still is, widely believed by millions of Americans.

Worse still, the prevailing misperceptions of the potential effects of radioactive fallout, and of nuclear war generally, as depicted in the Shute novel and elsewhere, have brought many of our countrymen to the equally false and even more dangerous belief that supremacy in nuclear forces is fundamentally meaningless and devoid of practical significance. What difference do numbers make, they reason, since *any* nuclear exchange, *regardless of which country might be ascendant,* would result in fallout and direct damage sufficient to cause the probable end of human life on earth and the near certain end of significant life in the warring countries.*

*A prime example of this type of rationalized disregard for the strategic imbalance is found as front page "news" in the *Washington Post* of Sunday, December 16, 1984. Under the headline "Relative U.S.-Soviet Strengths Change Little in 4 Years," Walter Pincus and Don Oberdorfer, after giving grossly incorrect and outdated data on the nuclear forces and defenses of the U.S. and USSR, add insouciantly that because nuclear war would be "holocaust", "the measurement of strategic power goes well beyond the sheer numbers, megatonnage, and delivery systems listed by 'nuclear accountants.'" (Apparently, the new pejorative "nuclear accountant" is to be used to discredit anyone not sufficiently terrorized by the prospect of Soviet attack to ignore the stark realities of American inferiority.)

Yet those who have studied nuclear effects most closely (and who have been required by their official position to examine the issue dispassionately) with virtual unanimity believe otherwise. In the words of Cresson H. Kearny, a Rhodes scholar and distinguished scientist who studied the effects of radioactive fallout for sixteen years as a senior staff member of the Oak Ridge National Nuclear Laboratory:

> "It would be far from the end of human life on earth. The dangers from nuclear weapons have been distorted and exaggerated, for varied reasons. These exaggerations have become demoralizing myths."

Nevertheless, as Kearney himself and other respected nuclear scientists like Dr. Edward Teller and Dr. Eugene Wigner have made abundantly clear, fallout does remain an incredibly terrible threat to the population of large portions of the United States, and neither these scientists nor we attempt to dismiss its dangers by the simple assertion that its effects are not as catastrophically annihilating or as long lasting as is generally believed.

In truth, fallout casualties in an *unlimited* surprise nuclear attack on the United States would be enormous, numbering in the tens of millions, and *unlike in the Soviet Union*, these casualties would not be mitigated by massive civil defense of the type in place in the USSR or by the rapidly increasing Soviet capability to destroy U.S. missiles *before* they can detonate inside the Soviet Union.

As a result, the devastating potential of radioactive fallout against Americans must not be ignored—either by erroneously concluding that life in the United States (and even the world) would end and therefore that the nuclear imbalance favoring Russia is immaterial; or with equal error by deciding that fallout would be only a minor subsidiary effect of a nuclear attack without major independent significance. With this realization and the rejection of the two extremes, the question then becomes not whether fallout ends the world or is insignificant but how best to avoid it entirely.

Safety rests on three conditions, each weakened if unsupported by the others.

First, radioactive fallout can be avoided *ab initio* by avoiding nuclear attack; and viable deterrent forces are the only secure means for preventing a Soviet first strike. The effects of fallout, like the other devastating effects of nuclear explosions, are far too horrible to entrust to Soviet goodwill or promises. We must accordingly do *whatever is necessary* to restore our own nuclear deterrent as the primary step and first line of defense in avoiding fallout.

Second, radioactive fallout can be curtailed, should deterrence fail, by developing active defenses—*as the Soviets are doing*—to destroy incoming nuclear weapons before they can explode. This second approach is obviously much less desirable than avoiding attack altogether through firm deterrence, but it is considerably better than docilely allowing Soviet nuclear weapons to fall on our heads when, through superior technology, they could be destroyed in flight or, in some instances, on the ground while being readied for launch. Additionally, the existence of active defenses would in itself greatly multiply the military potential and thus the political, preventive value of our deterrent *offensive* forces by protecting those forces as well as the population, thereby enhancing the deterrent effect of our weapons by making them able to survive a surprise attack.

Third, radioactive fallout could be greatly limited in its potential for national damage through basic measures of passive civil defense. Sound plans for the evacuation of cities and the sheltering of the population could reduce enormously potential fallout casualties since, because of the rapidity of radioactive decay, in a matter of days the worst dangers from fallout come to an end.

Knowing this to be a fact, *Russia has already spent more than 100 billion dollars for capital investment in civil defense and continues to spend at least five billion dollars per year to provide passive protection to Soviet citizens.* The United States has spent in the past, and spends today, effectively nothing. That failure greatly increases the real risk of war because Soviet civil defenses have become so formidable over time that the USSR may now be far more willing to attack than before, knowing that their own casualties would be relatively low while ours, at present, could be staggering.

The situation is summarized by Dr. Edward Teller:

"The Russians, having learned a bitter lesson in the second world war, have bent every effort to defend their people under all circumstances. They are spending several billion dollars per year on this activity. They have effective plans to evacuate their cities before they let loose a nuclear strike. They have strong shelters for the people who must remain in the cities. They are building up protected food reserves to tide them over a critical period.

"All this may mean that in a nuclear exchange, which we must try to avoid or to deter, the Russian deaths would probably not exceed ten million. Tragic as such a figure is, the Russian nation would survive. If they succeed in eliminating the United States they can commandeer food, machinery and manpower from the rest of the world. They would have attained their goal: world domination."

* * * *

"With relatively inexpensive governmental guidance and supplies, an educated American public could, indeed, defend itself. We could survive a nuclear war and remain a nation.

"This is an all-important goal. Its most practical aspect lies in the fact that the men in the Kremlin are cautious. *If they cannot count on destroying us they probably will never launch their nuclear arsenal against us.* Civil defense is at once the most peaceful and the most effective deterrent of nuclear war."

Nonetheless, funding for civil defense in the United States, including natural disasters, is only about 50 cents per year per capita whereas *Switzerland* spends almost $11 and the USSR about $20 . . . or, in other words, forty times as much *each year* to protect Soviet citizens as is spent by our Government to protect Americans.

This latter fact, coupled with the great, relentless multiplication of new Soviet warheads aimed at North America, led Cresson Kearney in 1980 to conclude:

"The ratio of American to Russian casualties in nuclear war could be 20 to 1 by 1985."

If Kearney is even approximately correct (and there is every reason to suspect he is), then the risk of war, or of the belligerent use of Soviet power in demanding concessions, could be approaching an unprecedented high. In these circumstances, the solution is not to ignore the problem by refusing to face it on grounds that the subject matter itself is too awful to contemplate. The proper solution is instead to examine the policies which have allowed our deterrent to erode and thus endanger our lives and independence and to take immediate corrective steps in our thoughts and perceptions and in our actions.

Unfortunately, as is increasingly becoming the case with our deterrent offensive forces and our developmental active anti-nuclear defenses, American civil defense is effectively non-existent. Reestablishing it will be hard.

Yet we cannot wait for the problem to go away; it is coming, not going. We cannot say it is too awful to contemplate, as if we were watching someone *else* drowning in a roaring river: we are in the river and our attention to saving ourselves should be fully focused.

In these conditions, the Federal Emergency Management Agency (FEMA) has made a few faint-hearted attempts to inform Americans about how to protect themselves from fallout and other nuclear effects, but our very limited protective and instructional efforts, by comparison with those of the Russians, border on the ludicrous. This self-destructive policy of silence, inaction, and even tacit deception of the public continues because, again in the authoritative words of Cresson Kearney:

> "Most defense planners do not believe that Americans could adjust to the actual danger which confronts them . . . This is unfortunate because the American public deserves to know the truth."

"Nuclear Winter"

Another fear that is widespread in America is the fear of a "nuclear winter." This theory was advanced by Carl Sagan who also espouses the marxist-related view that man is no more than a randomly selected composition of "star dust." The theory suggests that the smoke and dust from a global nuclear exchange would unbalance the world weather system and cause the world to freeze. As a theory, it is based on a number of assumptions, each one of which Dr. Sagan deliberately made the "worst case" from the perspective of world survival.

As a result, the "nuclear winter" theory only works if there is, for example, no rain, the oceans are not considered a source of heat, and the sun does not move in relation to the earth. These conditions have not been observed to occur in the past, and there is no reason to believe they will occur in the immediate future.

Moreover, events in *observed* nature tend to discredit even further Dr. Sagan's bizarre concept. First, in 1883, the Indonesian volcano Krakatoa exploded with a blast equivalent to 10,000 megatons of nuclear power, a detonation roughly equal to the entire global nuclear arsenal. The weather effect of this cataclysmic explosion with its millions of tons of debris (an entire island) scattered widely in the stratosphere was negligible. Similarly, a large meteor hit Siberia in the late 19th century and exploded with an estimated force equivalent to tens of thousands of megatons. The explosion ignited forest fires over vast areas, poured tons of smoke and dust into the upper atmosphere, but caused no major discernable effect on weather. Finally, when the Manicouagan meteor struck Quebec it created a crater 62 kilometers in diameter and exploded with the equivalent force of 17.5 *million* megatons of nuclear yield or more than *800* times the total explosive power of all existing nuclear weapons, yet the world continued.

Undeterred by these inconsistencies, two of Dr. Sagan's closest associates in conceiving "nuclear winter," Richard Turco and O. Brian Toon, served as members of the Pentagon-sponsored Committee on the Atmospheric Effects of Nuclear Explosions and greatly influenced the Committee's original draft report (October, 1983) on Sagan's theory. As a result, at least half of the twenty-six "referees" in the academic community who were asked to read the draft responded negatively.

One Committee member who served with Turco and Toon, Dr. Jonathan Katz, said that he and other scientists had objected to the first draft because it had "drastically overstated" the possibility of "nuclear winter" and that the comments of the outside reviewers were "as critical as any I've ever seen on a study like this." Because of the depth of the criticism, the report was, according to Dr. Katz, "totally rewritten," a fact little reported in the Press.

Dr. Katz and other knowledgeable authorities believe that Sagan has oversimplified the problem (perhaps to achieve a desired political objective) and that his book *The Cold and the Dark* is, in Dr. Katz's words, "recklessly iresponsible" in drawing "far reaching conclusions from uncertain evidence."

The pre-eminent physicist Dr. Edward Teller warned Congress on October 10, 1984, that the "nuclear winter" theory "is an unwarranted exaggeration . . . such predictions have proved *false* in connection with fallout and the depletion of the ozone layer which have been well publicized and discussed in the past." Finally, Dr. Teller pointed out that "nuclear winter" was receiving very little public notice in Russia in contrast to media attention in the U.S. and that recent valid research (by Cess, Potter, and Gates) which *admitted* the existence of rain, the warmth of the oceans, and the movement of the sun did *not* support Dr. Sagan's contrived formulation.

Nonetheless, at least one widely-read columnist is already claiming that, after an exchange of nuclear arsenals, the effect of "nuclear winter" would cause anything remotely like civilization to cease to exist in the Northern Hemisphere.

Completely overlooked, in the goal of spreading irrational fears which divert from the *justifiable* fears we ought to address, is the present *reality* that the Soviets can destroy the entire U.S. land based missile force with only a *small part* of their nuclear arsenal; that all of our nuclear warheads thus destroyed could never be detonated; that the Soviets are developing the capability to destroy U.S. sea-launched ballistic nuclear missiles high in the air *before* they explode; and that they are developing the "look-down-shoot-down" capability to destroy low flying U.S. cruise missiles also before detonation.

Unfettered by worries over "nuclear winter" or other unproven and suspect theories, the Soviet goal is to achieve the capability of being able to win a nuclear war in which only a part of the existing nuclear arsenals would be exploded—and that part would be mostly theirs . . . and the smoke and dust mostly elsewhere.

The progress they are making toward achieving that goal is made clear in the preceding "box scores" and general analysis.

CHAPTER I

Dreamland—1985

*"The people are tired, tired of noise, tired of incon-
venience, tired of greatness and longing for a place
where the world is quiet and where all trouble seems
dead leaves, and spent waves riot in doubtful dreams
of dreams."*

Walter Lippman, about
England in 1934

Great Britain fought World War I at great cost and, much
as the United States after World War II, thought she had won.
Seven hundred thousand husbands, sons, and brothers be-
neath the soil of Flanders' fields, no home untouched by grief
and no house without the vacant room, the loss of an Empire
set irrevocably in motion, a national economy never again set
right and soon devastated by Depression and ever rising welfare spending . . . these, not victory, were the simple English
realities of the 1920's and 1930's, these were the truths that
Englishmen sought ardently to deny, to minimize, or to forget.

The Conservative dominated Government of Stanley Baldwin, reelected in the Spring of 1935, had campaigned on a
chorus of renewed optimism and from the first days of reaf-
firmed Conservative power never saw its mission as that of
dispelling the persistent English dream of world peace with
an unchallenged Britain at the heart of a new global era of
harmony and prosperity.

But all the world was not England.

The long summer dream of war-wearied Englishmen counted
little with Hitler or Stalin. And yet, regardless of the vigor
of the occasional effort, England refused to be roused from
slumber and remained steadfast in what Winston Churchill
explained as a "period of exhaustion which has been described
as Peace."

Undeterred but isolated in that fact-denying dreamworld
of an exhausted people, Winston Churchill insisted on the
truth, demanded the truth, incessantly repeated the truth,
and told a nation sick of war that without preparedness for
war there would inevitably be war; that Nazi Germany was
engaged in a massive military buildup of then unprecedented
proportions; that English defenses were in a shambles; and
that continued English inaction invited attack, an abrupt

awakening, and untold suffering and misery repeating again the very tragedy England so desperately wished to forget.

Churchill's lonely efforts are now the documented history of the Stanley Baldwin-Neville Chamberlain era, but *at the time*, for his political honesty (which he no doubt viewed as public duty), Churchill was denied high government office, excluded from the Baldwin cabinet, and relegated to a position of isolated opposition within his own Conservative Party.

As early as 1929, Churchill had warned that the disarmament agreements of the post-war years were a disgraceful subterfuge which would give England a false sense of security, would be ignored by Germany, and would eventually invite attack. Churchill's arguments were dismissed as those of an anachronistic super-patriot out of tune with the times. In order to satisfy treaty-mandated arms limitations, the reduction of the Royal Navy (which within only a few years was required to borrow ships from the United States) continued unabated.

In 1931, surveying the continuing decline of British forces, Churchill urged full-scale rearmament with the plea that "England's hour of weakness is Europe's hour of danger." To an unimaginative and predominantly uninterested electorate, he characterized the British Army as "cut to the bone" and as no more than "a glorified police force." He hounded the public and the press with evidence of RAF failures, of Royal Navy shipbuilding fiascos, of service lethargy, of mismanagement in lieu of leadership, and of shortsighted planning instead of decisive action.

But Churchill's drumbeat of fact was suppressed, ignored, or, when acknowledged at all, treated as no more than the occasional ramblings of a maverick politician clearly out of the mainstream of even his own governing Conservative Party whose leading members perceived as a higher goal than the truth the necessity to appear "credible" and "moderate" and not in any case unduly to arouse the people in areas in which the people might demand "imprudent" action.

So Churchill, who sought to prevent war through preparedness for war, was called "immoderate" and even a "warmonger"—that most feared charge that can ever be leveled at any politician. And the great Conservative Party ostracized its greatest leader, treated him with indulgent and disdainful humor (if not with open scorn) and thought him unsophisticated and untutored in the complex ways of modern diplomacy, the practice and subtlety of which they alone could fully comprehend.

The dreams of dreams—the promises of safety through negotiation with Nazi tyranny—were cleverly constructed and in the public mind became real and even rational through the fatigued desires of a nation which craved escape from leadership, which closed its eyes to the grotesque face of the emerging enemy, and which welcomed the satisfaction of peaceful sleep.

But those dreams were forever shattered on the 1939 morning of the Soviet-Nazi invasion of Poland. England awakened that morning to more than the aroma of coffee. It was to the smell of blood and the taste of tears.

★ ★ ★

Today, Americans, if no longer dreaming, are certainly as lulled by the depth of slumber as any Englishman of the 1930's. And even if there should be this day an American awakening, rather than in six months, a year, or a decade hence, the bitter dawn for our country could bring an ultimate outcome far more devastating that that faced by an awakened England in 1939. Our choice on that day could be between suicidal resistance or phased surrender with ever increasing American subservience to Soviet will—a long evening before a longer night.

The advances of technology stimulated by World War II—mass instantaneous communication, world-wide rapid transportation, electronic archives, high speed data processing, nuclear weapons, chemical and now biological weapons, the explosion of high paced social change, and the general acceleration of history itself—have made effective control of all the lands and peoples of the earth, including the United States (indeed, especially the United States), an *achievable* objective. That was not the case in 1939, but regrettably it now is—for a power willing to invest enough, to be brutal enough, and (because there are people who feel that despotic powers care about the opinions of those they crush) to be shameless enough.

And now, there are no front line states that must be sacrificed to the aggressor while we leap to arms from troubled sleep. No Phillippines, no France, no Britain between us and Russia. The submarines are off *our* coasts, and the missiles will pass all the ancient buffer states swift and deadly in the cold of space. We are the front-line. There is no fortress

America—no arsenal of democracy—to rescue America as America rescued Britain.

Against that background, Soviet military power is rapidly approaching levels at which the observed progress of history toward Soviet global dominance already may have become irreversible. And the choices which may face an awakened America will be far more dangerous than those facing post-Victorian England in her dealing with a rearmed and aggressive Germany.

During this decade and possibly this year, Americans could face, and probably will be required to confront, in one form or another, the choice of incredibly perilous resistance to or docile acceptance of a new Communist dark age made possible by the technological acceleration of history, the weight of Soviet arms, and the new capacities for governmental control. This country was settled by people who wanted to have done with wars and empires: understandably, virtually all Americans want to deny the possibility of that choice and *either* of the potential results; however, continued disregard for the unsettling facts of the massive Soviet buildup and our own extreme vulnerability will only ensure an eventual day of reckoning *on terms far worse than those we refuse to face today*.

Awakenings come, to all but those who perish in their sleep: the question is when, and how harshly. But in our awakening, whether now or later, when we do rouse to consciousness, we are guaranteed to start from a position of substantial disadvantage and risk both because of the tragic folly of our past inaction and because Communist leaders in the Soviet Union already believe, for reasons few Americans have been told, that they have final global victory within their grasp. That is why any American attempt to regain strategic equality (much less superiority)—or to regain even that degree of lesser inferiority which Jimmy Carter euphemistically described as "essential equivalence"—could prove unacceptably dangerous: because we have so far to go and because the Soviet leadership will not willingly or easily give up to a seriously rearming America the decisive margin of military superiority the USSR presently holds.

And there can be little doubt but that Soviet Russia does believe that the point of no return in the strategic dynamic has indeed passed and that the Communist advantage is now irreversibly established. Even allowing for substantial Soviet propaganda and disinformation, there is ample valid evidence that the Soviets interpret the existing military realities as proof that their relative dominance can only increase. Repeated statements by their highest officials, almost all unreported by the American news media, attest to that unsettling fact.

The May 1972 issue of *Kommunist*, the Soviet Communist Party ideological journal, advised the West (much as similar Nazi publications did during the Hitler era):

"The military technical policy of the CPSU [Communist Party of the Soviet Union] is directed toward creating and maintaining *military superiority*."

And, as early as March, 1975, the Soviet Defense Minister, Marshal Grechko stated flatly:

"The correlation of forces has changed in favor of socialism and to the detriment of imperialism."

That same year, Soviet Foreign Minister Anatoly Gromyko made this stark announcement to Western diplomats:

"The present *marked preponderance* enjoyed by the forces of peace and progress gives the Soviet bloc *the opportunity to lay down the direction of international politics*."

These remarks were ratified by the 1977 Communist Party Program for the Soviet Union which declared:

"On the basis of *fundamental changes* in the balance of forces in the world, a *profound restructuring* of the entire system of international relations is taking place."

And, also in 1977, Soviet General H. Trofimenko, expanding Marshal Grechko's reasonings, was authorized to write:

"The change in the correlation of forces in the world (i.e., *the strategic nuclear balance*) is in favor of socialism."

This pattern continued until 1978 when the then Chief of the Soviet General Staff, Marshal Nicolai Orgarkov, finally took off the gloves and told a startled group of U.S. Congressmen visiting Moscow:

"Today, the Soviet Union has military superiority over the U.S. *Henceforth, the United States will be threatened. It had better get used to it.*"

But on the chance there should be any lingering doubt, the Soviet military journal, *Red Star* (January, 1980) gave Americans a final assessment:

"With respect to the military balance, the correlation of forces has shifted—*once and for all and irrevocably.*"

More ominously, the general tenor of the Soviet assessment has been repeated by our own experts and leaders whose strategic analysis, like that of the Soviets, only rarely has been reported to the American public.

For one example, as recently as May 24, 1984, our own Secretary of Defense, Caspar Weinberger, acknowledged publicly that "the Soviet military buildup, both quantitative and qualitative, has produced a *major shift* in the nuclear *and* conventional balance." This blunt admission by a U.S. Secretary of Defense was essentially ignored by the American press and television networks, who triggered no "missile gap" political controversy comparable to that of 1960 when the U.S. enjoyed overwhelming nuclear superiority, yet the entire country reacted with unrestrained disapproval of deficiencies reported in just one sub-category of weapons.*

The difference now is simple: in 1960 the American news media saw an obligation to inform the public about subjects involving the *relative* military power of the United States and its potential foes; today, the emphasis of the mass media has been to report *United States* military power either in a vacuum as if we alone had weapons or in relation *not* to the forces of our chief opponent but rather in juxtaposition to "hunger in America", "toxic waste," and the Federal deficit.

Speaking in 1974, Walter Cronkite of CBS News, with unusual candor, explained the news media policy:

"There are always groups in Washington expressing views of alarm over the state of our defenses. *We don't carry those stories.* The story is that there are those who want *to cut* defense spending."

*Intermediate Range Ballistic Missiles.

Venerated as Mr. Cronkite may be, the American public deserves better. We need to know why our defense forces are needed, and we especially need to know our relative military strength in relation to our adversary's even if an accurate accounting of that status does not fit media preconceptions or plans for the redirection of American society.*

Moreover, when the Government underestimates or underpublicizes Soviet strength, the news media have a special obligation in our democracy to bring the facts before the public. With few exceptions, that obligation, also, has not been discharged.

Here again the situation is not unlike the news media failure to alert the public to the dangers of German militarism in the days prior to World War II.

As Winston Churchill stated in May, 1935:

> "I am astounded at the indifference with which the Press ... seem to view the fact that the Government have been utterly wrong about German ... strength."

But even on those rare occasions when our Government and Government officials have openly warned of the enormous growth in Soviet strength, the news media in America have treated those warnings with studied indifference.

Accordingly, here from official statements and publications we extract some of the many essentially unreported, yet significant statements which reflect how far the Soviets have progressed toward attaining the goal for which they have striven at unbelievable cost, sacrifice, and suffering.

That goal, in almost every respect, parallels the goal of Hitler's massive military preparations prior to World War II. Therefore, we should consider carefully the implications of these official warnings for our own time and future.

The Joint Chiefs of Staff in the Fiscal Year 1985 Military Posture Statement:

> "The Soviets have now developed strategic offensive *and defensive* capabilities that *erode the credibility* of the U.S.

---

*Perhaps with that thought in mind Fairness in Media, under the relevant provisions of the Securities Act, has initiated a public solicitation of the purchase of CBS common stock, presumably to work against the prejudices of that and other television networks through shareholder voting power.

deterrent and *increase the risk* that Soviet leaders would consider launching a surprise nuclear attack. . . . The Soviets hold a *distinct advantage* in terms of total numbers of strategic offensive forces . . . The Soviets have a *survivable* superior offensive capability. . . . Soviet strategic forces are *more effective* than those of the United States."

President Reagan, March 31, 1982:*

"The Soviet Union does have *a definite margin of superiority*—enough so that there is risk."

President Reagan, March 23, 1983:

"The Soviets have enough accurate and powerful nuclear weapons to destroy *virtually all of our missiles on the ground* . . . The Soviets have a present margin of superiority."

The Secretary of Defense, Caspar Weinberger, in the Fiscal Year 1984 Defense Posture Statement:

"The Soviets have acquired a margin of nuclear superiority in most important categories."

The Joint Chiefs of Staff, in the Fiscal Year 1984 Defense Posture Statement:

"Over the past two decades, the balance of strategic nuclear power has *shifted steadily* toward the Soviet Union."

U.S. Department of Defense, *Soviet Military Power*, 1983:

"The global military balance has been shifting steadily against the U.S. and its allies."

---

*President Reagan and Secretary Weinberger have on frequent occasion tried to warn of the tremendous growth in Soviet power but neither have met with notable success because of the hostility of the news media, their own pedestrian bureaucracies, and, we suspect, the crushing weight of their day-by-day responsibilities. Similar attempts have been made repeatedly under similar adverse conditions by the Secretaries of the Army, the Navy, and the Air Force, by Under Secretary of Defense Iklé, and by Assistant Secretary of Defense Perle.

U.S. Air Force message to Congress, in April 1984:

"There is a *destabilizing* imbalance between U.S. and Soviet strategic forces [in favor of the Soviet Union]. . . ."

Richard De Lauer, Under Secretary of Defense, on March 9, 1983:

"They've [the Soviets] got superiority now. . . ."

In July, 1980, the Republican Party Platform and the ensuing Presidential Campaign highlighted the dangers of Soviet strategic supremacy. The Platform read:

". . . Since 1977, the U.S. has moved from essential equivalence to *inferiority* in strategic nuclear forces with the Soviet Union . . . that inferiority invites *diplomatic blackmail* and *coercion* of the U.S.

"The evidence of the Soviet threat to American security has never been more stark and unambiguous . . . *America is in danger without parallel since December 7, 1941.*"

Yet despite that initial concise statement of crisis (and despite later underpublicized official acknowledgments of growing American inferiority), because of Congressional success in blocking the Reagan plan for restoring American defenses and because of news media success in creating, at the same time, the erroneous impression of a major *American* defense buildup, the relative superiority of Soviet power actually has greatly *increased* since the Republican victory of November, 1980.*

Unfortunately, the Republican Party Platform of 1984 was not as candid as that of 1980, and at a political level, during the 1984 election year, there was strong pressure to blur the truth and claim major defense posture improvements rather

*An August, 1984 poll conducted by Opinion Research, Inc. disclosed that 60% of the American public now believes that the United States has military superiority over the Soviet Union. In 1980, a majority of Americans recognized the severe weaknesses of our defense. This reversal of public opinion, while the trend against our security has actually accelerated, is a tribute to the power of the news media to misinform, especially when coupled with unabashed political puffery claiming success for failure.

than to place the blame for failure where it belongs—on Congress and on an irresponsible mass media. In fact, for differing reasons—mostly related to self-interest—almost no one in public life has been willing to admit freely that under a Republican Administration *the chief defense accomplishment has been only to slow—and only slightly—the rate of our decline.*

Senator John Tower, recently retired as Chairman of the Senate Committee on Armed Forces, has been one clear exception. On April 3, 1984, Senator Tower bluntly told the Senate that because of Congressional opposition, all that the Reagan defense program had been able actually to accomplish was *to slow the rate of growth of Soviet military superiority* and that *"the imbalances" favoring Russia would "continue to widen."*

In contrasting Senator Tower's frank and truthful warning with the fatuous and ill-informed norm in American political pronouncements, we are reminded of what Winston Churchill told the British Parliament in 1932:

> "I cannot recall any time when the gap between the kind of words which statesmen use and what is actually happening . . . is so great as it is now. The habit of saying smooth things and uttering pious platitudes and sentiments to gain applause, *without relation to the underlying facts*, is more pronounced now than it has been in my experience."

And his remarks later in 1933:

> "*Unless the people know the truth, one day they are going to have a very surprising awakening.* Not to have an adequate defense in the present state of the world is to compromise the foundations of national freedom and independence."

Yet, like Winston Churchill before him, Senator Tower's warnings seem to have fallen on deaf ears.

CHAPTER II

Two Roads to Tyranny

—Soviet Preparations for Global Victory—

"Is it possible to transmit the experience of those who have suffered to those who have yet to suffer? Can one part of humanity learn from the bitter experience of another? Is it possible to warn someone of danger? Your proud skyscrapers point to the sky and say: it will never happen here. It's not possible here.

It can happen. It is possible. As a Russian proverb says: 'When it happens to you you will know it's true.' Do we have to wait until the knife is at our throats? Isn't it possible to assess the menace that threatens to swallow the whole world?"

Aleksandr Solzhenitsyn,
Russian Novelist and Patriot

For several decades most Americans have instinctively recognized that the Soviet Union is exactly "the evil empire" of Ronald Reagan's rhetoric. Indeed, few Americans doubt that the Soviet Union is now, and long has been, striving for world dictatorship as a founding step for world Communism.

So the problem for our democracy and for freedom in America is not in a lack of public recognition that Communism is undesirable nor is it in any extensive public unawareness of the general Soviet intention to achieve global dominance. The fundamental problem *is*, however, an almost complete failure on our part to comprehend (or unwillingness to accept as fact) the enormous Soviet geopolitical and military advances which have occurred in the span of only the last few years. And that failure is coupled with and magnified by an equally astonishing American inability to perceive clearly the marked recent acceleration of power *loss* by the Western democracies and power *gain* by the Socialist dictatorships.

Americans also have been persuaded by endless news media misrepresentations that Soviet leaders, like American politicians, view strategic military power simply as a means for deterring attack (as is the view in our country). But the harsh truth is that Soviet leaders, as their own statements attest, see strategic power much more broadly: first, as a means of coercing geopolitical gains by openly displaying the *capability* to wage and *win* strategic war and, second, as a means, if necessary, of *forcing* geopolitical gains by actually attacking and *winning* in strategic battle.

Thus, while America seeks only to maintain a strategic deterrent (exclusively nuclear) strictly to *prevent* attack, the Soviet Union as a matter of state policy seeks strategic power (nuclear, chemical, biological and anti-nuclear defensive) at those *superior* levels necessary not just to deter attack but to gain the advantages of being able to *fight and win* intercontinental war. And that precise Soviet policy is abundantly evident both from repeated Soviet statements confirming their belief in victory in total strategic conflict (and in the coercive utility of having the option) and from the kinds and structure of Soviet offensive and defensive strategic forces which *go far beyond those reasonably needed to deter an essentially unaggressive America.*

To an American public long indoctrinated by news media coverage in the belief that nuclear war is unwinnable, the hard fact that Soviet leaders believe the exact opposite is indeed sobering. And regardless of whether the American news media or the Soviets have the more accurate view, it is the Soviets who can control or unleash their massive nuclear superiority, not Walter Cronkite.

But how did the Soviet Union reach its present position of superiority and why have American leaders accepted inferiority? The story is a saddening one, but it must be understood to appreciate the full extent of our tragic decline.

Now long ago, in the early days of the development of atomic weapons, American scientists faced, as many saw it, a serious dilemma: how to guarantee that there would never be a nuclear war and, as seen by some of the scientists, how to prevent the United States from using its monopoly of nuclear weapons to enforce its will unjustly on other world nations, including the Soviet Union.

Those scientists most worried about the latter prospect solved it through treason—by delivering wholesale the fruits of American atomic research to the Soviet Union (or to England and thence the Soviet Union). Those remaining scientists, more worried about global peace, were thus given a basis for their own role in the process of eliminating the possibility of a nuclear Pax Americana—that role was the development of a world plan allegedly for averting nuclear war (now that two antagonistic powers were nuclear armed) grounded in the notion that each power would hold the population of the other hostage to nuclear attack so that *neither* could afford to strike.

This ingenious proposal, developed during the late 1940s and 1950s by academicians and nuclear scientists, was called the doctrine of Mutual Assured Destruction (MAD). Its theory has been perhaps best described by Robert Jastrow, the founder of the NASA Institute for Space Studies, and himself an early developer of nuclear weapons and close confident of Dr. Robert Oppenheimer, Dr. Harold Brown, and the other scientist-authors of MAD.

Dr. Jastrow explains:

"The premise of Mutual Assured Destruction is that the Soviet Union will be deterred from a surprise nuclear attack on the United States by the knowledge that such an attack would trigger a devastating American counterattack. And, of course, *we* are deterred from an attack on the USSR by the knowledge that the Soviets maintain a similar arsenal. The result is a nuclear standoff, and world peace."

But something was seriously amiss. Dr. Jastrow explains further, with considerable frankness:

"The trouble is that MAD is a theory, and like all theories, it depends on an assumption. *This assumption has turned out to be false* . . . It is now clear [in 1983]—in fact it has been clear for a decade—that while for many years the American government adopted the strategy of Mutual Assured Destruction proposed by our scientists and academicians, the Soviet government rejected it. The USSR undertook to do exactly what our strategists say it is supposed not to do: it implemented large programs for defending its citizens from nuclear attack, for shooting down American missiles, and for fighting and winning a nuclear war. The result, as Senator Moynihan has said, is a 'policy in ruins and *the greatest peril our nation has faced in its 200 year history*'."

But why, after the true intentions of the Soviets became clear—indeed were made clear with brutal directness—did our leaders, unlike Dr. Jastrow, continue (and why do they still continue) to cling to the doctrine of mutual assured destruction?

First, our leaders have simply not been able or willing to accept that Soviet statements about strategic war actually reflect Soviet belief . . . and indeed reflect a large degree of realism. Thus just as the British politicians of the 1930's refused to take at face value Hitler's clear-cut statements of aggressive intent and in fact went to extraordinary lengths to apologize for his intemperate and bellicose words and even for his actions in secretly arming Germany, so too have the American politicians of the 1970's and 1980's tried to explain away repeated Soviet declarations of *their* intent, if necessary, to fight and win nuclear war and have likewise attempted to minimize *Soviet* actions in building, often in secret, the necessary forces to have that exact ability.

But since any politician trying to bring attention to stated Soviet war-winning doctrine (and to their matching strategic forces) runs a high risk of being subtly labeled a warmonger by the American news media, the result is that probably not more than one American citizen in a thousand is aware of the full implications of Soviet declarations like those which follow.*

Voyennaya Mysl (an internal publication of the *Stavka*, or Soviet General Staff, quoted in the USAF publication *Soviet Military Thought*):

> "The most important task of the Soviet General staff in preparing for a modern war is the detailed planning of employment of nuclear weapons by all services of the armed forces."

Voyennaya Strategiys ("Soviet Military Strategy", p. 193):

> "The armed forces of the Soviet Union . . . must be prepared above all to wage war under conditions of the mass use of nuclear weapons . . . the basic method of waging war will be massed nuclear rocket attack."

*These statements by the Soviets about their own policies call to mind this passage from John Lothrop Motley's *Rise of the Dutch Republic:* "Tyranny, ever young and ever old, constantly reproducing itself with the same imposing mask which it has worn through all the ages, can never be too minutely examined, *especially when it paints its own portrait,* and when the secret history of its guilt is furnished by the confessions of its lovers . . . the perusal of its traits will not make us love liberty the less."

Marxism-Leninism on War and Army (translated from Russian in the U.S. Air Force publication, *Soviet Military Thought*):

"Nuclear missile strikes . . . and the ability to use them *before* the opponent does, are the key to victory."

The Offensive (translated from Russian in the U.S. Air Force publication, *Soviet Military Thought*):

"It is recommended that the Soviet strike be launched . . . *unexpectedly* for the enemy. Preemption in launching a nuclear strike is expected to be *the decisive condition* for the attainment of superiority."

Chilling? Yes. Acknowledged in American politics? Hardly ever. Reported by the U.S. news media? Never.

Yet there is a second reason, or rather explanation, for the incredible failure of most American leaders to recognize, or if they recognize it, to acknowledge openly, true Soviet objectives and for the continued silence of these leaders in the face of hard facts. It is, quite plainly, that we and they have been hoodwinked, bluffed, lied to, and generally outwitted by the Soviet Union. These deceptions occurred throughout the critical period of "detente" and during the ensuing miasma and myopia of arms limitation treaty negotiations, particularly those carried under the general rubric "Strategic Arm Limitation Talks" or SALT.

In its major aspects the process began in 1967, when the then Secretary of Defense, Robert McNamara, first left U.S. Armed Forces bogged down in a deliberately indecisive war in Vietnam and then *froze* U.S. strategic force levels. Excepting the *downward* variation under President Reagan, *those strategic force levels have remained fundamentally the same ever since.*

In other words, since 1967, the United States has essentially observed, and has done so unilaterally, the "nuclear freeze" about which Americans are now hearing so much, yet *Russia after 1967* unilaterally kept racing in an "arms race" without competition and kept right on building ICBMs, SLBMs, and bombers and spending over

$40 billion or more *each year* on nuclear warheads, missiles, and submarines.*

In retrospect, we realize McNamara's decision to freeze U.S. strategic forces has jeopardized our lives, our freedom, and even the very existence of the United States as an independent nation, yet at the time, McNamara's decision fit the Mutual Assured Destruction strategy of the Defense and State Department intellectuals like Dr. Harold Brown. In point of fact, Dr. McNamara's decision was in his day thought exceedingly wise, since the Department of State elite believed Russian belligerence would disappear once the Soviets "felt secure" with equality of forces.

And by 1969, the Russian build-up *did* reach a level of equality with the frozen U.S. forces. Concurrently, therefore, the Nixon Administration, impelled by the misguided judgments of Dr. Henry Kissinger, formulated the policy of detente, which derived from the premise that Russia would relax tensions now that peace through the doctrine of Mutual Assured Destruction was at last firmly at hand with nuclear equality on both sides and both populations fully hostage.

But again, notwithstanding our supplicating overtures of cooperation and coexistence, Russia continued building missiles, nuclear warheads, and submarines, and our government kept doing nothing except to plead even more ardently for negotiations and for the opportunity to make the Russians understand that, by our calculations, they already had all the weapons they could possibly need to make MAD work.

And Russia kept building.

In retrospect, detente was a mistake, Dr. Kissinger was wrong, and President Nixon greatly compounded the original McNamara error by trying to talk reason to the Soviets rather than explaining the hard facts to his countrymen and looking exclusively to our own American self-interest.

Yet unlike McNamara, Dr. Kissinger, to his credit, has openly *acknowledged* the failure of the policy he formulated and President Nixon implemented, providing us now this admission and warning:

*In fact, since we froze our intercontinental force levels in 1967 the Soviets have added approximately 1200 ICBM launchers (including SS-20 launchers), 950 SLBM launchers, and 380 intercontinental bombers.

"The 1980s could turn into a period of great instability . . . we could be heading into a *period of maximum peril* . . . by some time in the *early 1980s* the Soviet Union will have the capability to destroy with a reasonable degree of confidence most of our land-based ICBMs. In the same period of time we will not be able to destroy the Soviet ICBM force. This creates a gap in the design of the two forces that is bound to have a geopolitical consequence, *especially since we are clearly inferior in forces capable of local intervention* . . . the military balance is beginning to tilt ominously against the U.S. in too many significant categories of weapons. . . . *To conduct business as usual is to entrust one's destiny to the will of others* and to the self restraint of those whose ideology highlights the crucial role of the objective balance of forces. . . .Never in history has it happened that a nation achieved *superiority* in all significant weapons categories *without seeking to translate it at some point into some foreign policy benefit.*"

He had not been alone in making his mistakes: he was not alone in repenting them. As early as November 1978, William Hyland, one of Kissinger's senior assistants, grimly stated:

"We are already witnessing the *political consequences* resulting from a shift in the overall *military balance. . . .*"

"Detente," as a euphemism for appeasement, has been quietly returned to the French language from which it was unwisely borrowed, yet the tardy lamentations of Drs. Kissinger and Hyland, however welcome, are still hauntingly reminiscent of British experience in the 1930's. In 1934, the British Cabinet *also* admitted that England had disarmed to the edge of risk and had done so deliberately in pursuit of disarmament, but *as is the case today* that admission of error was *not* followed by corrective action.*

Thus Hyland's tacit acknowledgment of the failure of detente came *after* the fall of Indochina in 1975, Angola in 1976, and Ethiopia in 1977, but *before* the belated discovery of the

---

*Martin Gilbert, Churchill's official biographer, observes that when the British archives of the period were finally opened they revealed incredible duplicity even conspiracy by the government in concealing relevant data from the public.

Soviet combat brigade in Cuba in 1979, *before* the brutal Soviet invasion of Afghanistan in the same year, *before* the Soviet military intimidation of Poland in 1980-81, and *before* the Soviet-Cuban takeover of Nicaragua in 1979 and assault on El Salvador in 1980-81.

Against that dismal background of evident failure, a yet even more telling assessment of the damage done by Kissinger's policy of detente is not surprisingly found in this succinct analysis of Winston Churchill II, grandson of the great Prime Minister:

> "Henry Kissinger and Cyrus Vance . . . were babes in arms when it came to dealing with the Russians, and Kissinger has had the frankness to admit as much. For all these high-principled men's untiring efforts to secure effective strategic arms control agreements and to achieve a genuine detente, the harsh truth must be faced that, by the dawn of the eighties, the world has become an infinitely less secure place, aggression and bloodshed more rife, and the East-West balance more precarious with the Soviet Union disposing twice as many nuclear missiles as it had barely a decade before when the detente policy was being launched with such high hopes. *The deception of the peoples of the Western democracies by their leaders has been cynical and unforgivable, bringing the world to the point where all out war has become a serious possibility.*"

But most telling of all is this grim proof of Soviet duplicity and American stupidity provided direct from the mouth of the Soviet dictator Leonid Brezhnev, during a 1973 speech to Communist leaders in Prague:

> "We are achieving *with detente* what our predecessors have been unable to achieve using the fist . . . *By 1985* we will be able to extend our will wherever we wish."

The year is now 1985 . . . , but in 1972, Richard Nixon *believed* Dr. Kissinger's flawed advice and Richard Nixon *knew* that arms negotiations with Russia would play very well indeed in an election year news media that was busily doing its best to force negotiations by putting the political squeeze on the President and using the not unfamiliar technique of regularly depicting the President to the people as truculent and dangerously aggressive in his military policies.

How often must we see this process repeated? Is it to become a permanent feature of American Presidential elections with demands for concessions to the Soviets made more onerous in each election cycle?

The pattern is firmly in place, and in 1972, much as is being repeated now and was repeated in 1984, the President's political interests were allowed to prevail over the national interest, and the SALT agreements of 1972 launched America down the long road of negotiating and negotiating and negotiating, while Russia kept building and building and building, and American politicians, mouthing the platitudes of peace, kept talking and talking and talking, mostly to their own bored electorates, and mostly—let us charitably assume—not even themselves understanding what they have said.

Still, even allowing for the growing and almost expected mediocrity of most American politicians, why have virtually all American leaders, some of whom are brilliant men, watched silently while Russia achieved overwhelming military superiority essentially unchallenged? How in any rational system could our strategic nuclear forces have been kept frozen at the same overall basic level for eighteen years while Soviet nuclear, chemical, and biological forces have undergone explosive growth at as fast a rate as a self-strangulating Socialist economy could permit?

The first two answering ingredients are the steadfast American refusal to accept Soviet doctrine at face value coupled with the understandable but still inexcusable desire of politicians to appear forever blessed as "peacemakers" regardless of reality or public duty. A third equally important factor in what must be a composite answer is the unswerving pig-headedness of the American news media in permitting Soviet manipulation of its liberal political prejudices to achieve Soviet propaganda and disinformation objectives.

The 1981 KGB document authored by A. V. Kuznetsov and entitled *The Practice of Recruiting Americans* names "government officials with access to secret papers *and journalists*" at the top of its list of ten priority targets for Soviet recruitment. But actual Soviet agents in the American news media (and it would take the ultimate in naivete to believe there are none) are not the real difficulty; it is instead the astonishing unfamiliarity with military subjects displayed by most newsmen and their almost childlike devotion to the liberal mythology of the 1960's and its discredited thesis that the USSR has only defensive military goals.

A recent statistical survey by the prestigious America Enterprise Institute gives these revealing facts about the politics and prejudices of the American media elite:

- *96%* backed Lyndon Johnson over Barry Goldwater for President.

- *Seven to one* they agreed that their fellow-journalists were leftist.

- *Eight out of ten* admitted they voted for George McGovern whose unilateral disarmament and appeasement proposals caused him in 1972 to carry only the District of Columbia and Massachusetts.

There is little wonder then that established media outlets like the *New York Times, Washington Post,* and the national T.V. networks, together with their sycophantic following in the media "hinterland" (e.g. obscure smaller newspapers like the *Raleigh News and Observer*), are effectively devoid of information concerning Soviet actions which do not fit preconceived liberal notions.

Yet the final element comprising the reason for the still baffling American non-reaction to Soviet military superiority and to the continuing Soviet buildup is perhaps the most disheartening consideration of all. It is the abject failure of the United States Congress to face up to the realities of the greatest threat ever faced by our nation ... just as happened in Congress during the period prior to World War II.

This state of affairs continues to exist notwithstanding the hopes of millions that the 1980 elections would effect serious change in terms of defense policies. In practice, we have seen that the chief result of the major 1980 Congressional realignment has not been a more effective and informed Congress, only a more boring Congress.

As Winston Churchill told a similarly composed British Parliament in March, 1938:

"For *five years* I have talked to the House on these matters—not with very great success. I have watched this famous island descending incontinently, fecklessly, the stairway which leads to a dark gulf . . . Historians would never be able to understand it if mortal catastrophe were to overtake Britain. They would never understand how a victorious nation, with everything in hand, suffered themselves to be brought low, and to cast away all that they had gained by measureless sacrifice and absolute victory—gone with the wind . . . the burden in peacetime of taking the necessary and advised steps to defend the country was too great, for Britain to contemplate."

He sounded tired and not surprisingly. He had been even more direct, to no good purpose, sixteen months before:

"I have been staggered by the failure of the House of Commons to react effectively against these dangers. I would never have expected that we should have been allowed to go on getting into this plight, month by month, and year by year. Even the Government's own confessions of error have not produced a concentration of Parliamentary opinion and force capable of lifting our efforts to the level of emergency."

He had grounds to be staggered. The previous April he had urged:

"All threatened nations must act immediately and in concert in order to avoid a war which would not only destroy homes and lives, but reduce such civilization as we have been able to achieve to primordial pulp and squalor. *Never till now were great communities afforded such ample means of measuring their approaching agony. Never have they seemed less capable of taking effective measures to prevent it.* Chattering, busy, sporting, toiling, amused from day to day by headlines and from night to night by cinemas, they can yet feel themselves slipping, sinking, rolling backward to the age when the earth was void and darkness moved upon the face of the waters. Surely it is worth a supreme effort—the laying aside of every impediment, the clear-eyed facing of fundamental facts, the noble acceptance of risks inseparable from heroic endeavor—to control the hideous drift of events and arrest calamity upon the threshold. Stop it! Stop it! Stop it now! Now is the appointed time."

No great leader has come forward in the America of the 1980's to speak to our Congress, and to us, with such eloquence and with such force and candor.

That failure is *the most inexplicable factor* in attempting to answer why American leaders have watched in silence while their country becomes a second-rate power and our liberty a function of Soviet good will.

Yet is our decline exclusively the fault of our leaders? Is it exclusively the fault of the news media? Can we blame one single President, one single Congress, one single event, or one single decision? We cannot.

While descending, like England, our own "stairway that leads to a dark gulf," we ought to ask a far more fundamental question: what inherent American quality has made us seemingly incapable of recognizing our own perilous decline? How could this great and good nation in which so many hopes of mankind rightly rest have been launched in silence on this downward slide of which so few are even dimly aware? What in our national character is so terribly flawed that we would in ignorance and apathy accept the descent of this tragedy on ourselves and on the whole world?

Perhaps it is the well recognized American trait of ignoring responsibility until the hour of crisis. Perhaps it is our history of long years of security behind the profound protection of two oceans. Perhaps it is our still retained frontier openness which is always ready to find good will in nations as in men.

As a people, we have an unfortunate tendency to lack perseverance in protracted struggles and to ignore disappointments by turning our backs to unpleasant developments.

The great enthusiams of World War II carried forward into the post war era of confrontation with the Soviet Union. But by the late 1960's those energies had dissipated on the rocks and shoals of an indecisive war in Korea, the natural anxiety of the Cuban Missile Crisis, and the interminable morass of Vietnam. Additionally, Americans, who had staked so much on the "liberation" of European colonial empires and the expected emergence of new third-world democracies, soon saw those infant nations turn promptly to totalitarianism and anti-Americanism, and we felt betrayed by a world which accepted our largesse but viciously rejected our friendship and our governing system.

These experiences perhaps contributed to our unstated and largely unconscious decision to ignore Soviet military growth during the 1970's (and today) and to our tiring of competition with the USSR in world affairs. Tenacity over the long haul was never a prime American strength whereas, to the contrary, it has been the principal characteristic of Russian survival over centuries of threatened existence.

Yet even these perceptions of our national flaws do not explain fully the degree and disorienting speed of our decline.

This much only is certain. No one man, no one institution, and no one event has caused our downward progress. That has been consistently incremental, and it has been almost imperceptible as step by step we have gone our quiet way down the stairs.

In truth, therefore, none are blameworthy; all are blameworthy. This, our developing tragedy, may ultimately be a downfall in which the whole world must share, but it has been in its inception entirely of our own making.

As a result, two roads to world Soviet dominance are wide open. And we, Americans all, have issued the tempting invitation for their use.

Along one route—and the most easily and therefore the most likely to be traveled—the Soviet Union can use its still growing strategic superiority to coerce gradual Western acquiescence and surrender. To nudge America and the West along that path, the Soviets likely will continue low-intensity "wars of national liberation" in the remaining non-Communist authoritarian countries of the third world, will almost certainly increase covert tampering with the internal politics of democratic countries of the industrial West, and will even more openly demand Western arms limitation and disarmament with less and less regard for even the appearance of reciprocity.*

---

*At the time of this writing, there are emerging public indications that sometime in the summer of 1982 the United States accepted in secret an arms control agreement with the USSR within the framework of SALT II. What is known publically about the agreement indicates that the Soviets are excused from *any* specific overall limitations on Strategic Nuclear Delivery Vehicles (SNDV's) and possibly from any cap on nuclear systems with multiple independently targetable reentry vehicles. In contrast, the United States is held to both limits. In further contrast are these words of President Reagan spoken in the nationally televised debate of October 30, 1980: "SALT II is illegal because the law of the land, passed by Congress, says we can not accept a treaty in which we are not equal, and we're not equal in this treaty for one reason alone: our B-52 bombers are considered to be strategic weapons; their Backfire bombers are not."

Additionally, Soviet military superiority likely will be used with equal effect to encourage further concessions from the Western international financial institutions—the International Monetary Fund, the Inter-American Development Bank, the International Development Bank, the World Bank, the Asian Development Bank, and the lot—whereby significant portions of the amassed capital reserves of the West will be gradually transferred to the Eastern bloc to support balance of payment requirements arising largely from additional Soviet military investment.

Simultaneously, Soviet power could also be used to encourage continued Western lending to Socialist underdeveloped countries (UDCs) in order to deplete Western economic resources that might otherwise be available for Western rearmament and for supporting economic expansion in free enterprise economies. As a part of the latter process, Soviet military power may also eventually be used to back up resource-rich UDC's (e.g. Libya, Angola, Iran, etc.) in artificially driving up the price of natural resources thereby further weakening the Western free economies while increasing the requirement for *resource-poor* UDCs to finance high-priced imports on credit with ever additional demands on Western capital.

Already the Soviet military buildup has been greatly aided by Western financial assistance. Already Soviet demands for Western grain and technology appear to be satisfied in part from fear of the military repercussions which might follow denial. Japan, for example, has been on occasion notably helpful to Russia in supplying militarily useful technology, and some observers feel Japan has done so not as much for profit as to retain the good will of an awesomely powerful neighbor with large military forces immediately adjacent to the Japanese Home Islands. And grain sales and financing concessions to the USSR are already a fact of life all too well known as an American means of seeking Soviet favor and benign behavior.

Already, too, Soviet strategic power has been used to coerce partial nuclear disarmament in Europe. Largely as a result of the opinions and actions of U.S. Assistant Secretary of State for Europe (and former *New York Times* reporter) Richard Burt, just since the election of President Reagan, more than 1000 nuclear warheads have been *unilaterally withdrawn* from Europe and *under Soviet pressure* an additional 1400 are being withdrawn from European bases of the North Atlantic

Treaty Organization (NATO). In the same period, *even without counting reload missiles*, Russia has *added* at least 2,300 nuclear warheads aimed at NATO on the SS-20, SS-21, SS-22, SS-23, and SS-C-4 reloadable missile systems.*

Even the few (a dozen or so) new tactical U.S. ballistic missiles (Pershing IIs) recently introduced by NATO in Europe have only *replaced* one-for-one other comparable already deployed U.S. missiles, thus producing *no net numerical gain whatsoever* and far from offsetting the more fundamental (but little reported) appeasement of the USSR through the withdrawal of the 2,400 other nuclear weapons which have been, or are being, *removed but not replaced*. These 2,400 U.S. weapons are being withdrawn at least partially in response to the public warning issued by Soviet Dictator Chernenko in September, 1984, that West Germany would be safe from nuclear attack only if it gets rid of American nuclear missiles.**

In short, we are already seeing strong evidence that Russia is using military might to coerce Western compliance with Soviet will. And as Russian power increases, Russian willingness to take risks and make greater demands will undoubtedly increase as well.

Robert McFarlane, the President's National Security Advisor, recently pointed out in a speech to the Commonwealth Club of San Francisco that the Soviet adventurism of today in Angola, Ethiopia, South Yemen, Cambodia, Afghanistan, and Nicaragua would have posed unacceptable risks to Russia as recently as ten years ago when Soviet strategic nuclear supremacy was not yet established. McFarlane went on to explain that these risks were now acceptable to the Soviets because American unilateral nuclear reductions of "more than 25 percent" had been met by Soviet construction of "more than 10,800 additional nuclear weapons."

Obviously, however, the preferred choice of the Soviet Union is to take as few risks as necessary and to capture the people and wealth of the West intact. With massive and growing

---

*The SS-C-4 is the new Soviet ground launched cruise missile. Its range exceeds 3000 km.

**Chernenko's threat to West Germany was accompanied by a Soviet decision to arm *East* Germany with new SS-21 nuclear missiles and by the construction of new Czechoslovak bases for even additional short-range nuclear missiles aimed at the Germans and presumably the rest of Western Europe.

strategic superiority, the USSR is gaining the ability to curtail and even to forbid new Western military systems and demand yet further cuts in existing Western defenses—all as the Soviet Union travels the high road to achieving Western subjugation on the installment plan. Or, to repeat without apology—for they have not been quoted often enough—the succinct words of the deceased Soviet dictator, Leonid Brezhnev: "by 1985, we will be able to exert our will *wherever we wish.*"

Yet, there is also a second road to Soviet global dominance, a short-cut the Soviet leadership has never ruled out.

If the West should now belatedly decide to make a determined challenge to Soviet superiority—whether through development of high technology anti-nuclear defenses, through offensive nuclear rearmament, or through direct conventional opposition to some new Soviet aggression, perhaps in Iran or Pakistan—then Russia might feel *compelled* to use its present ability to defeat the West in nuclear battle. This second road, because of the tragedy of American inaction during the period of detente, is also wide open, and the great test of the free people of the world in the remaining years of the 1980's will be to find a way to close down the second road *completely* while successfully resisting the coercion and blandishments of the better traveled route.

Having understood these unhappy prospects for some time, Aleksandr Solzhenitsyn a few years ago made this prediction of how eventual Soviet victory would come about:

> "At one time there was no comparison between the strength of the USSR and yours. Then it became equal . . . [The Soviet advantage grew]. Then [it became] three to one. *Finally it will be five to one* . . . With such a nuclear superiority it will be possible to block the use of your weapons, and on some unlucky morning they will declare: 'Attention. We're marching our troops to Europe, and if you make a move, *we will annihilate you.*' And this ratio . . . of five to one will have its effect: *you will not make a move.*"

Today, the effective nuclear advantage of the USSR over the United States is 6 to 1 *and growing.*

In this circumstance, we could profitably recall again the wisdom of Winston Churchill, who said in September, 1938, to the British Parliament:

"Owing to the neglect of our defenses . . . we seem to be very near the bleak choice between War and Shame. My feeling is that we shall choose Shame, and then have War thrown in a little later, on even more adverse terms than the present."

We must avoid the choice Churchill accurately predicted for England. We must avoid choosing either shame or war by choosing neither.

CHAPTER III

Disasters of Good Will

—The Role of Arms Control in Increasing the Risk of Nuclear War—

"Soviet arms control [SALT II] compliance will be assured by our own nation's means of verification . . . were the Soviets to take the enormous risk of trying to violate the treaty in any way that might affect the strategic balance, there is no doubt that we would discover it in time to respond fully and effectively."

Jimmy Carter, Message to
the Senate, June, 1979

"I will spit in your eyes, and you will say it is Holy Water."

Russian Proverb

Americans are an amiable people. We instinctively understand and feel deep cultural affinity for Will Rogers' sentiment, "I never met a man I didn't like."

From our position of vibrant economic activity, of great national wealth and personal comfort, of long life expectancy and apparent domestic wellbeing, we have been, with the exception of those very few who have seen briefly the rigors of combat, a people essentially insulated from the immediacy of death and the day-by-day struggle for life. No nation in our hemisphere has ever even remotely approached our military strength, and we have extended our will in the Americas not by seizing territory but through the immensity of our economic and cultural power. We have been amply able to afford the luxury of good will toward all men.

Russia is an open plain swept for centuries by arctic winds and invading armies. Russia has met the problems of its long history through force, guile, deception, and conquest in countless twilight wars with violent enemies of equivalent strength. Tyranny, death, famine and disease: these have been the ever-present companions of the Russian nation. Insulated from nothing, suffering and hardship have been the watchwords of daily life and the will to prevail against all adversity, the required and absolute condition of national character.

And yet they have understood us, while we have failed to understand them. They have perceived our amiability, our guileless honesty, and our self-satisfied and self-satisfying yearning for the good. They have understood our indifferent and almost casual good will toward a world outside our happy frontiers engaged in the daily struggle to survive, and they have forged that knowledge into their greatest weapon in confronting what they view as their last and greatest enemy.

That weapon has nowhere been used to greater success than in the deceptions of "mutual" arms control and disarmament. Endlessly, American good will has trusted Russia, accepted Russian excuses, sought out Russia, offered Russia concession after concession, and accepted every Russian fault and lie while demanding from itself, from its own people and government, the highest standards of honesty, good faith, and faithfulness.

But the bloom is perhaps at long last off the rose. Decades of Russia cheating America, of taking America for every advantage, are beginning to tell even on us, to take their measure even on our seemingly boundless reservoir of good faith.

Yet the full realization that Russia has indeed taken us for little more than well-fed fools is impeded by another long-standing American trait: the inability to admit error.

Now that our government does in fact see more clearly the full implications of Soviet use of arms control negotiations to delay and terminate American defense programs, now that wholesale Soviet violations of treaty obligations can no longer be ignored, and now that Soviet strategic supremacy is an accepted fact in high political circles, our leaders are still reluctant to admit to themselves and to the American people the full truth of the success of Soviet deception and duplicity or the bitter results of our own mistaken trustfulness.

Accordingly, the U.S. Department of State still imposes on the Department of Defense a bankrupt policy of unilateral American compliance with the unratified SALT II Treaty and does so notwithstanding incontrovertible proof of massive Soviet violations. Accordingly, even now at the time of this writing, Assistant Secretary of State Richard Burt (former correspondent wiith *The New York Times*) is urging President Reagan to postpone reporting additional Soviet arms control violations to Congress and to accept a "moratorium" on developing and testing anti-nuclear space defenses until 1990, both actions ostensibly to encourage negotiation of a prohibition on anti-satellite weapons which, if ever negotiated, Russia would certainly ignore and the U.S. would scrupulously obey.

Accordingly too, virtually every American politician from Presidential candidate to Clerk of the Probate Court still feels compelled to sing hymns of praise and highest hosannas at the altar of the failed and false God of arms control, even at a time when no rational man can believe that Russia will adhere to any agreement with the United States.

And nowhere in any public forum is recalled Lenin's warning of *eighty years ago:* "Let the hypocritical or sentimental bourgeoise dream of disarmament. We must strive, not for disarmament, but for the universal arming of the people."

Against these obvious truths—even told to us by our adversaries, the depth of our continued folly in grasping at the straw of negotiated security is indeed unfathomable, but we must, nevertheless, try to understand. The unseemliness of our diplomats and arms control disciples in clinging to every excuse for Soviet duplicity (and barbarity) must be brought to a quick end, but it can only be ended through a better knowledge of the precise motive and beliefs of these poorly informed Americans who have so much control of our fate. We must attain that knowledge since they are, and will likely remain, in the positions of power, and they must be persuaded to see the danger if *we* are to have any hope for their dealing with Russia on a sane basis while sufficient time remains. A first step is greater public awareness of the extent of Soviet deceptions, of how the process has evolved, so that the public will be in a position to impress the importance of the facts on our leaders.

Fortunately, during the Reagan Administration, some progress has grudgingly occurred in providing us with information on Soviet duplicity and in groping toward realistic assessments of Soviet use of negotiating strategies and deceptions to impede American defense programs and thus to accelerate the relative growth of Soviet supremacy.

For example, the Department of Defense in April 1984 did cautiously advise Americans as follows in its official publication *Soviet Military Power*:

"To the Soviets, treaties are *manipulated* in the manner most conducive to the interests of national policy objectives."

Yet even that carefully phrased official statement was a pale reflection of the more forthright and helpful analysis of President Reagan himself who on January 29, 1981, put the matter to the American people in somewhat more straightforward language:

"The Soviets reserve unto themselves the right to commit any crime, to lie, and to cheat."

And with equal bluntness directed toward those who insist that with patience (isn't almost seventy years enough?) Soviet behavior can be modified, President Reagan responded in October, 1983, soon after the Russians murdered the passengers on the civilian airliner KAL 007:

"We cannot change the Soviets, yet we *can* change our attitudes toward them. We *can* stop fooling ourselves that they dream the same dreams and cherish the same hope that we do."

Nevertheless, despite these and the President's frequent other efforts to speak the hard truth, the Department of State on countless fronts does *not* change its attitude of always favoring conciliation toward the USSR and *we* do continue fooling ourselves in myriad ways by accepting virtually every proffered excuse for Soviet militarism and imperial growth.

What in the nature of democracy has made this drive for self-delusion so overpowering? How can President Reagan, who stated in January, 1980, that "the Soviets only see weakness in a President (i.e. Carter) who clings to the unilateral observance of the fatally flawed SALT II Treaty" and, later in the same year, that "I can not agree to any treaty, including the SALT II Treaty, which in effect legitimizes the continuation of a one-sided [Soviet] arms build-up," *also* state in a formal message to Congress in January, *1984*, that "the United States will continue to comply with SALT II"? What about our system makes so compelling the acceptance of these inconsistencies and the exhaltation of unending fatuity?

Perhaps the answer is two-fold: perhaps the pressures of democracy to paint an always rosy picture and to describe an atmosphere of harmony and compromise, even with tyranny, are irresistably overwhelming ... and are so until the tyrant's knife is not just at the throat, as now, but actually in the jugular, as is surely coming. Perhaps also the tyrant's already superior power demands compromise of truth to purchase the temporary illusion of security, albeit false and gained at the price of secretly coerced appeasement.

Again, modern history is the best guide in understanding the disheartening process in which government leaders may occasionally speak the truth but in which they rarely act upon it. Again, as a prime example, no one now can doubt that British government in the 1930's, regardless of governing political party, consistently refused to support or even propose adequate spending for defense against the growing Nazi military buildup *even while admitting the Nazi menace*. They too preferred the continued pretense of negotiated security instead.

Here is one retrospective British explanation offered in the case of one such government which describes why the completely honest course was not taken and never deemed politically feasible:

> "It may be said that the Prime Minister Neville Chamberlain and the Government ought not to have accepted this atmosphere of 'business as usual' in the face of the Nazi build up. Yet what could they have done in the circumstances? To have *frightened the country* into immediate war measures might, in the Autumn of 1938, have destroyed *the hope* of any result from the Munich agreement. I doubt whether even Churchill, if he had been a member of the Government, could have *roused the country* in the Spring and Summer of 1939 to an all-out war effort . . . It needed the explosions of Dunkirk and the Battle of Britain to dissipate once and for all *the misty atmosphere of peace* and to give the nation a clear view of the needs and dangers that faced it."
>
> Sir Samuel Hoare, 1954

The foregoing analysis is confirmed by a prior admission of Prime Minister Stanley Baldwin (Chamberlain's predecessor) who blandly confessed to putting the political interests of his governing Conservative Party ahead of the national interest:

> "Supposing I had gone to the country and said that Germany was rearming and that we must rearm, does anybody think that this pacific democracy would have rallied to that cry at that moment? I could not think of anything

that would have made *the loss of the election* from my point of view more certain."

No politician, even the brave, wishes to risk defeat by dispelling "the misty atmosphere of peace." Only Churchill, a rarity missing today, had enough confidence in himself and in freedom to "tell the truth to the people . . . they are tough and robust."

Yet in Stanley Baldwin and Neville Chamberlain's time, as now in that of President Reagan, there was—besides the distasteful chore of leveling with the public—another even more difficult consideration at work. In Chamberlain's case particularly, that factor was the very real effect of existing and growing Nazi military potential on the negotiating process itself.

Using that potential to the fullest, Hitler compelled the 1938 Munich negotiations. Once at Munich, he was able eventually to coerce a negotiated result which has become a symbol for appeasement. He was able to do so because Churchill's warnings of 1929 and 1930 were a forgotten echo, because Churchill's pleas of 1935 and 1936 had gone unheard, and because Churchill could find *for England* no solace or strength in his earlier correct prediction of German military superiority *over England*.

Ultimately, beyond the eleventh hour, on October 6, 1938, even Neville Chamberlain himself finally admitted before the very outbreak of World War II that the British Government policy of minimal national defense and maximum reliance on negotiation was in ruins. He acknowledged specifically that German military supremacy had in fact *coerced* diplomatic appeasement:

> "Our past experience has shown us only too clearly that weakness in armed strength means weakness in diplomacy."*

A brief review of the enormous American disadvantage reflected in the Box Scores (pp 00 to 00) thus leads to an inevitable uncertainty: whether President Reagan, a man of far stronger character than Neville Chamberlain, has also been

---

*A degree of similar belated recognition is found in a recent statement of U.S. Secretary of State George Shultz: "Arms control will simply not survive in conditions of inequality." (Department of State, May 14, 1984.)

forced to a position of weakness in diplomacy because of "weakness in armed strength."

Yet how else can our President's total reversal of position on SALT II be rationalized? How else can be explained American compliance with an unequal treaty called "fatally flawed" by the President and, worse still, now known to be routinely violated by the Soviet Union?

Unilateral compliance with SALT II under these circumstances is at the very least a strong indicator that the President *does* feel heavily burdened in diplomacy by the weight of Soviet strategic arms in the global balance. Moreover, as a further result of that burden, his political advisors may find the President *even more open* to the political inducements of favorable press coverage and public popularity gained through increasingly frequent Munich-style pronouncements so high-sounding in the ears of the electorate and the press . . . even those matching Neville Chamberlain's ill fated remark, "I believe that we shall have peace in our time."

Whether the appeasement elements of the present Administration will continue to prevail (as they did in Britain until Dunkirk) is still, regrettably, an open and crucial question. In seeking an answer, some in our government still recall and find a source of hope in the simple realism of the President's 1964 declaration concerning Communism:

"We are at war with the most dangerous enemy that has ever faced mankind."

And in his resolve expressed twenty years later on November 29, 1984:

"We are determined that we are not going to let them maintain or enlarge their superiority in weapons . . . we are determined not to let them maintain or continue that lead."

But words alone are not going to suffice. Unfortunately too, the appeasement faction and the self-styled pragmatists among the President's advisors, not to mention the arms control fanatics in Congress and at the Department of State, invariably find *their* recommendations for *disarmament* supported enthusiastically by the national news media which can make the most incredible folly appear wise and cause the most extreme position to be deemed moderate. But even more unfortunate, and hard though it may be to explain, the press-favored positions of acquiescence and accommodation to the Soviets are supported, not infrequently, by individuals in the Department of Defense as well.*

Not unlike the British forces of the 1930's, the bureaucrats at the U.S. Department of Defense on far too many occasions still seek to curry favor with the press and the politicians by denigrating the significance of the wide disparity in military force between the United States and the USSR, usually while asserting that simple force comparisons and the alarming imbalances they reveal are not realistic evidence of relative strength and do not imply "lack of parity."

No doubt there will be those at the Department of Defense who will challenge the data presented in this study *even though* the data is drawn *from* the Department of Defense and other Defense agencies. If so, these official critics can be expected to assert (as has been their general rule when confronted with similar analysis in the past) that "all relevant factors" have not been taken into account and that "although the trends are ominous" there is "no present cause for concern."

That approach, which surfaces with great regularity, and especially in Congressional testimony, is starkly similar to that taken by military men in England in the days before their hour of greatest peril.

In this 1934 statement of the British Air Staff, consider the striking parallel between British military thinking in the 1930's and frequently professed American military thinking today:

> "There is no ground for alarm at the existing situation. Whatever first-line strength Germany might claim, we remain today substantially stronger if all relevant factors are taken into account. But the future, as opposed to the present, may cause grave concern."

One historian of that period, Professor Harold Rood, quoted the following example to illustrate the underlying purpose (and indeed also the cause) for the never-never land quality of contemporary British military thought in the mid-1930's:

---

*The present Chairman of the Joint Chiefs of Staff is *not* one of them and has been outspokenly candid in his presentations to Congress and to the people, thus being largely ignored by the news media.

"As for defense, it was agreed that the Royal Air Force's notion of possessing *air parity* with the German Air Force was *not* to be taken to mean that Britain would have an air force of *equal* size and striking power to that of Germany, but rather that 'parity' should be defined as 'effective deterrent strength,' a euphemism meant to disarm those who thought the air force under strength for its task of defending the homeland."

Similarly, that same desire to disarm those "alarmists" acquainted with the facts and the same wishful thinking necessary to cause every assumption to favor one's own forces and disfavor those of the opponent were also, as with us today, pervasive factors influencing and distorting pre-World War II British intelligence estimates. Those estimates, we now know, almost invariably *understated* Nazi forces, intentions, and capabilities.

Here again, in our time and circumstance, American intelligence all too often also shows a virtually identical form of institutional bias which persistently downplays Soviet military accomplishments or tends to cloak in unnecessary secrecy the size of Soviet forces and the extent of their treaty violations. This current bias is most often manifested by a frame of reference in which the present must always be described as benign, even if the future may be admitted as ominous. "All relevant factors" becomes the measuring phrase for the avoidance of hard reality and for the introduction of irrelevant subsidiary assumptions.

This process of covering up or explaining away strategic realities was described *but not excused* by its chief British opponent, Winston Churchill, in words holding equal validity if applied today to America and to many American leaders:

"We must regard as deeply blameworthy before history the conduct . . . of all democratic leaders, *both in and out of office,* during this fatal period. Delight in smooth-sounding platitudes, refusal to face unpleasant facts, *desire for popularity and electoral success irrespective of the vital interests of the State,* genuine love of peace and pathetic belief that love alone can be its sole foundation, obvious lack of intellectual vigour . . . all of these constituted a picture of British fatuity and fecklessness which, though devoid of guile, was not devoid of guilt, and, though free from wickedness or evil design, played a definite part in the unleashing upon the world the horrors and miseries, which, even so far as they have unfolded, are beyond comparison in human experience."

But startling as these parallels are, there is today one critical difference. Again, as Dr. Harold Rood, Professor Emeritis of Political Science at Pomona College warns us:

"The situation in which the United States finds itself today is *not* that of Britain with its Churchill to hold the fort while we Americans get half ready. There is no American Empire to which the U.S. fleet my retreat while the other democracies of the world prepare to deal with the foe. *There will be no distant and protected arsenal of democracy upon which the United States can draw to remedy these deficiencies in military strength created by the disbelief in war or the unwillingness to see the menace.*"

Professor Rood adds this further observation:

"Debates on military matters in the United States do not turn on questions about American capability to *win* a war, but on the *assumption* that there will not be one."

Yet in the Soviet Union, on military matters, there are few platitudes, no inquiring electorate to be disarmed disingenuously through euphemism, and *never* an assumption that there will be no war. With distressing clarity, the Russian General Staff publication *Soviet Military Strategy* states:

". . . The Soviet government . . . and their armed forces must be ready *primarily* for a *world war* . . . the Armed Forces of the Soviet Union . . . must be prepared above all to wage war under conditions of the *mass use of nuclear weapons* . . . the preparation and waging of just such a war must be regarded as the *main task* of the theory of military strategy and strategic leadership . . . Creating the *advantage* over the enemy in nuclear weapons and methods of their use is *the most important task* in the building up of the armed forces in peacetime as well as during the course of war."

94

The obvious benefits of strategic superiority are openly acknowledged and further extolled in the authoritative Soviet armed forces journal *Military Thought*:

"*Superiority* accelerates the process of the *physical and moral defeat* of the enemy, makes it possible to operate more daringly and decisively, and to impose one's will on the enemy and to attack him more successfully. Superiority:

- promotes the development of flexibility in the selection of scales, forms and methods of conducting combat operations;

- expands the scope of methods for coordinating the delivery of *nuclear*, fire [artillery], and air attacks with the maneuver of troops; and

- increases the effectiveness of using space, time, and other factors which influence the course of military operations."

Yet the *only* authoritative American governmental or political document of recent time to call openly for American strategic superiority was the 1980 Republican platform on which Ronald Reagan was overwhelmingly elected. It read as follows:

"We will build toward a sustained defense expenditure sufficient to close the gap with the Soviets, and ultimately reach the position of military superiority that the American people demand . . . The general principles and goals of this stragegy [of peace through strength] would be . . . to achieve overall military and technological superiority over the Soviet Union."

The 1984 Republican Platform, perhaps in part because of the growing pressures of Soviet military power, contains no similar commitment. That omission, reflecting both a failure of will and strategic perception, occured despite warnings similar to those we have previously noted, including the important statement of Senator John Tower, who when Chairman of the Senate Committee on Armed Services, formally acknowledged on April 13, 1984, that with respect to American strategic *inferiority*:

"The current imbalance will continue to *widen*."

Also distressingly absent from the 1984 Republican Platform is any clear commitment to inform the American public as to the full scope of Soviet arms control violations and strategic deceptions. In contrast, the 1980 Platform read:

"The Republican Party deplores the attempts of the Carter Administration to cover up Soviet non-compliance with arms control agreements . . . We pledge to end the cover up of Soviet violations of SALT I and II, to end the cover up of Soviet violation of the Biological Warfare Convention, and to end the cover-up of Soviet use of gas and chemical weapons in Afghanistan and elsewhere."

Yet, not until more than *three years later,* on January 23, 1984, did the current Administration formally report to Congress, and to the people, on *any* Soviet arms control violations and, according to Congressional testimony of Assistant Defense Secretary Richard Perle, the report finally issued was "illustrative only" and "twenty to twenty-five" more Soviet violations remained to be publicly revealed.

Nonetheless, President Reagan's January, 1984 Report was an important step toward fulfilling the 1980 pledge to end the Soviet violations cover-up by the Carter-Mondale Administration. The fact that the Report was rendered *at all* is historic and unprecedented. For the first time in our history, an American President openly accused the Soviet Union of violating Strategic Arms Limitation commitments. That accusation, made by formal message to Congress, is irrevocable and though woefully incomplete, must be applauded.

The President's report to Congress embodied the full consensus of the national security and intelligence agencies, and it revealed that the Soviet Union had violated *six* different arms control agreements in *nine* different cases, including two violations related to SALT II obligations, which were declared clearcut, unqualified, and unequivocal:

"The United States Government has determined that the Soviet Union is violating:

1. The Geneva Protocol on Chemical Weapons;
2. The Biological Weapons Convention;
3. The Helsinki Final Act;
4. telemetry encryption [SALT II] and;
5. a rule concerning ICBM modernization [SALT II].

"In addition, we have determined that the Soviet Union:

6. has almost certainly violated the ABM Treaty [SALT I];
7. probably violated the SALT II limit on new types [of ICBMs];
8. probably violated the SS-16 [ICBM] deployment prohibition of SALT II;
9. and is likely to have violated the nuclear testing yield limit of the Threshold Test Ban Treaty."

Worth noting is that a total of four of the nine cited violations relate to the critical strategic nuclear limitations of SALT II. And SALT II is the proposal on which America has based, and mistakenly continues to stake, its primary national security interest hinging on nuclear deterrence. As noted, of these four critical violations of SALT II, the President considers two of them as having been proven conclusively.

In that regard, worth noting also is this official statement from the Department of Defense:

"Several of these violations must have been planned by Soviet authorities many years ago, in some cases perhaps *at the very time the Soviet Union entered into the agreements."*

Moreover, in March, 1984, the Senate was told by a former member of the Joint Chiefs of Staff and by other witnesses that twelve years before, in 1972, neither the Senate nor the Joint Chiefs were informed of vital intelligence information that the Soviet Union intended to violate the SALT I Accords even before they were signed. Through an inordinate and even irrational desire to appear before the public as peacemakers

*The bewilderment and dismayed innocence of this realization is met and overmatched by Lenin's cynicism of 1916: "Every peace program is a deception . . . unless its principal object is . . . the revolutionary struggle."

and to preclude jeopardizing the chances of SALT I approval and thus electoral success, the Nixon Administration apparently withheld this essential military intelligence from our top military leaders who, remaining in ignorance of it, supported SALT I as did a similarly uninformed Congress.

In particular, and according to at least one Senator respected for his expertise in arms control, Dr. Henry Kissinger may have deliberately misled the Senate by failing to reveal our knowledge of a Soviet plan for circumvention of the key SALT I provision limiting heavy ICBMs. If so, SALT I and the whole ensuing fabric of strategic arms control since 1972 received Congressional approval at its inception under false pretenses covering-up Soviet bad faith. In any event, no one can now doubt that Russia *from the beginning planned to use the agreed limitations of SALT to freeze U.S. defenses while illegally building Soviet might.* Any other interpretation ignores the facts of Soviet strategic growth and what they have themselves revealed. As the Soviet foreign policy expert, Rostislav Tumkovskiy, wrote in 1979 for internal Soviet readership only:

> "Signing the [SALT I] agreement was a *victory* of the Soviet Union in the arms race."

But we Americans have sadly still not learned from our mistakes, nor will we readily admit them, and the January 1984 Report on Soviet arms control violations shows little more than the tip of the iceberg. Much of the hidden bulk below the surface is contained in a classified study* prepared by the President's General Advisory Committee on Arms Control (GAC) which is publicly reported to have stated in November, 1983:

> "Aspects of Soviet conduct related to about *half* their documentary arms control commitments were found to constitute material breaches of contracted duties."

Public accounts also indicate that the additional Soviet arms control treaty violations *confirmed* by the "GAC Report" are, as follows:

---

*An abbreviated, unclassified version of this study was released on October 10, 1984, at the insistence of several Senators and Representatives.

1. Soviet circumvention defeating the object and purpose of the 1972 SALT I Interim Agreement through deployment of their medium SS-17 ICBMs and their *heavy* SS-19 ICBMs to replace illegally their light SS-11 ICBMs.

2. Illegal tests of surface to air missiles and radars in a prohibited anti-ballistic missile (ABM) mode in violation of the SALT I ABM Treaty.

3. Breach of the Nuclear Test Ban Moratorium an atmospheric nuclear tests through Soviet atmospheric testing breakout.

4. Breach of the Kennedy-Khrushchev Agreement of 1962, by deploying offensive (possibly nuclear and probably chemical and biological) weapons in Cuba.

5. Breach of the Limited Test Ban Treaty of 1963, through 31 ventings of radioactive debris beyond the borders of the USSR.

6. Breach of the Montreux Convention of 1936, by illegally sending aircraft carriers to and from the Black Sea through the Dardanelles.

7. Breach of the SALT I Interim Agreement and the ABM Treaty of 1972, involving widespread camouflage, concealment, cover and deception.

8. Breach of the SALT I Interim Agreement, involving excess ballistic missile launchers.

9. Breach of the SALT I ABM Treaty, involving the ABM-3 movable radar currently in mass production and initial deployment.

10. Breach of the 1981 Conventional Weapons Convention, by illegal use of fragmentation and incendiary weapons of mass destruction in Afghanistan.

11. Total disregard for the 1982 commitment to a Moratorium on SS-20 ballistic missile deployment, by continuing deployment.

12. Completely violating fundamental SALT II commitments by massive increases in strategic camouflage, concealment, and deception as well as by active interference with American national technical means of compliance verification.

In sum, there are apparently a total of 21 Soviet arms control treaty violations *already confirmed by the President himself* or *by the President's General Advisory Committee*. Moreover, besides official confirmation, the existence of each violation is supported by much other credible evidence as well.

Further, in addition to the officially confirmed breaches, there is evidence of 17 *even additional* remaining Soviet SALT violations, and for each of these there is also strong supporting evidence. These violations are awaiting confirmation by the President.*

Already, however, Assistant Secretary of Defense Richard Perle has told Congress (February 20, 1985):

"The Soviet Union has violated *almost all* of the most important arms control agreements signed since 1963."

Finally, a full catalogue of Soviet deceit shows there are a total of over 310 cases of Soviet arms control and other diplomatic deceptions since the Bolshevik Revolution of 1917. *Fifty* Soviet Treaty violations involving international security have been confirmed by *official* Defense and State Department reports (ignored by the news media) and by Senate studies. In fact, official U.S. government documentation now fully supports the conclusion that the *Soviets have violated, evaded, or circumvented virtually every international treaty they have signed since 1917.* (See Appendix II.) In fact, the only significant treaty the Soviets are known to have *kept* was their agreement with Hitler to invade and divide Poland, the event which precipitated World War II.

In 1934, Winston Churchill challenged the British Government to explain to the English people and the world that the Germans were violating the arms control provisions of the Versailles Treaty. In the House of Commons, Churchill stated:

*As this publication went to press, a large number of these additional violations were confirmed by the President in a message to Congress dated February 1, 1985.

"The worst crime is not to tell the truth to the public . . ."

Unfortunately, the British Government lied to the British people. Thus Britain slept until Englishmen had the choice of another World War or eventual Nazi domination.

To avoid a similar choice, we must first admit to ourselves the true result of our misguided recent history. We must acknowledge that the hypnotic fog of detente has frozen U.S. forces and brought about *de facto* unilateral American disarmament through stagnation and obsolescence of U.S. strategic systems and the corresponding massive growth in the quality and quantity of Soviet weapons. Additionally, countless successful Soviet deceptions and the hidden practical military effects of Soviet arms control violations have further aggravated the strategic imbalance —an imbalance which never more urgently required the American government to take countermeasures than it does now. These are the concrete realities we must face.

We must recognize also that overdue remedies will not be cheap.

Former Carter Administration Defense Secretary Harold Brown said in 1979 that, without SALT, the United States would be required to spend 30 to 100 billion dollars more on defense during the 1980's for strategic systems. Now that massive Soviet violations have made SALT, which already favored the USSR, a mere hollow shell, America must accept the new reality and must implement defense programs—even, as Harold Brown said, at the additional cost of tens of billions of tax dollars—in order to achieve any hope of catching up with Russia, much less regaining our lost superiority. Yet the Reagan Administration has been forced by Congress to spend tens of billions of dollars *less* on defense than proposed *even by Jimmy Carter,** whose defense program relied on Soviet good faith and on Soviet SALT compliance.

To build public and Congressional support for the strategic spending that even the Carter Administration admitted would be needed (and that most Americans even now erroneously believe is being expended), American leaders must come clean with the American people and explain the effect and extent

---

*See Box Score Number Nine.

of Congressional defense budget cuts as well as the full extent and effect of Soviet arms control breakout; otherwise, Americans could receive a highly unpleasant surprise when finally given an answer to Professor Harold Rood's question:

"Can it really be true that Soviet negotiations for the Strategic Arms Limitation Treaties are nothing more than part of the preparations for war? That would place Soviet leaders in no better odor than Adolf Hitler . . ."

CHAPTER IV

Sword in the Balance

—The Use of Soviet Power to Mold American Behavior—

"Until at last not only Rome's resources but her spirit failed her also . . . and so the Senate foregathered, and bade the generals find some way of inducing the invader to depart . . . and a treaty was made . . . that they should deliver a thousand pounds weight of gold to Brennus King of the Gauls who should rule both nations thereafter. And upon this wicked and humiliating settlement, the invader's insolence heaped another injury: for when the gold was to be weighed he would have it measured in his own lying scales: and when the Roman general refused, the Gaul flung his sword into the false balance 'that they might pay all and the sword's weight, too.' And they say a voice was heard that the Romans could not endure hearing, crying 'Conquered! Woe to thee, thou art Conquered!'

But Camillus [outside the City] bade them recover their country with iron not gold, having before them the temples of their gods, their wives, their children, and the land where they were born."

Livy, *History of Rome,* describing events of 390 B.C.*

Allen Drury, in the best selling 1983 novel *Hill of Summer,* adopted in fiction the premise that the USSR had achieved such enormous military preponderance that it could confront an American President with the choice of bending to Soviet will or risking defeat in nuclear war. Worldwide Soviet naval and military maneuvers, a squadron of Soviet ballistic missile submarines deployed to Cuba, these and other provocations underlined the seriousness of the intention of the Soviet Union to impose its will in a fictional U.S.-USSR confrontation in the year 1985. In these circumstances, the protagonist of Drury's novel, a newly inaugurated American President, relies on Red China for help and is promptly double-crossed.

---

*Rendered by Timothy Dickenson from John Bellenden's 1533 translation of Livy from Latin to Scots. (W. Blackwood & Sons, London, 1901.)

Hill of Summer is fiction. Its fundamental thesis of Soviet coercion is emerging fact. To understand why, we should examine recent *actual* events.

On April 2, 1984, the Soviet Union initiated, without warning, a total world-wide deployment of its entire Navy. Ballistic missile submarines, aircraft carriers, naval aircraft, surface combatants of every type were all put to sea and in the air under conditions simulating preparation for a general nuclear war. The rare public accounts of this occurrence (buried generally in the overall deafening silence of the American news media) indicated that U.S. intelligence was caught completely by surprise, not only by lack of any forewarning of the exercise, but also by its enormous scale. In the words of one U.S. official, "if it floated, it went to sea, and we were caught with no warning . . . the whole thing was not just impressive, *it was intimidating.*"

But there was more to come. Immediately after demonstrating the ability to put the largest Navy in the world entirely at sea in a matter of hours with no warning, the Soviets calmly launched from an operational (*not test*) Strategic Missile Regiment a salvo of six SS-20 ballistic missiles on a trajectory *aimed at the United States.* In mid-flight, the Soviet missiles were brought down short, somewhere in the Barents Sea, but the underlying message of the mock nuclear attack could not have been lost on our American leaders.

That message is simple. The Soviet Union is increasingly contemptuous of America and American forces. The Soviet Union is on perpetual war footing and is not afraid to threaten the use of power or to use power to see its will prevail. The Soviet Union expects and will increasingly demand changes in American behavior to reflect better the new reality in which the correlation of forces has shifted "once and for all and irrevocably" in favor of Russia.

A book authored in 1982 by the then Chief of the Soviet General Staff, Marshal Ogarkov, entitled *Always in Readiness to Defend the Homeland,* is also *not fiction.* Yet Marshal Ogarkov's book contained statements of policy which foreshadowed the April, 1984 provocations and which amply confirm the plausibility of Alan Drury's fictional theme in *Hill of Summer.* Ogarkov stated:

". . . The task of achieving continuous preparedness for *the immediate mobilization deployment of troops and na-*

val forces, prompt and expeditious shifting of the Armed Forces and the entire national economy from a peacetime to *war footing*, is assuming particular national importance. The question of prompt expeditious shifting of Armed Forces and the entire national economy to a *war footing* and their *mobiliization deployment in a short period of time* is much more critical today."

To which the Marshall added a uniquely Soviet view of negotiations with the West:

"We should accompany our [negotiating] steps *with maximum military preparedness.*"

These ominous directives are consistent with the long-standing Soviet belief that military supremacy is indispensable to eventual Communist global dominance. As Soviet Marshal V. D. Sokolovsky stated sixteen years ago in the baseline doctrinal work, *Soviet Military Strategy*:

"The creation and constant maintenance of quantitative and qualitative *superiority* over the enemy in the nuclear means of armed conflict . . . is the most important problem of building modern armed forces."

But today, the problem for America is not just that the Soviets have now achieved their objective of strategic supremacy but that they are evidencing an ever-growing propensity to *employ* strategic supremacy to assert their will.

Consider the following examples of Soviet provocative behavior in recent months which ought to demand our attention, which no doubt have gained the secret attention of our leaders, but which the American news media with studied imperception failed to cover.

- During 1984, the Soviets conducted unprecedented, gigantic land military and supporting naval exercises aimed at intimidating subjugated Poland, neutral Sweden, and pro-Western Japan. These exercises have been entirely offensive in character, targeted against nations which pose no threat whatsoever to the Soviet Union. Although Russia conducts exercises each year, these maneuvers were *not routine*. Their purposes appear to include political coercion, testing of U.S. early warning and intelligence capabilities, desensitization of pro-Western leaders and publics to provocative Soviet military actions, and, possibly, actual preparations and practice for general war.

- Throughout 1983-1984, the Soviets intensified their campaign of military threats and pressure against our NATO allies. This campaign is designed to induce the European members of NATO to distance themselves from the United States or to threaten to distance themselves from the United States in order to pressure us in turn to make our own concessions to the Soviets.

In addition to the large scale maneuvers already described, other incidents have occurred:

- The Soviets have made numerous recent specific threats to NATO and the United States in response to the NATO Euromissile deployments (Pershing II and GLCM) and have remained opposed to removing their outrageous preconditions for resuming Intermediate Nuclear Forces (INF) and Strategic Arms Reduction (START) negotiations.

- In further response to the limited U.S. Euromissile deployments, they have made good their threat to deploy long-range cruise missile submarines immediately off the Atlantic and Pacific coasts of the United States and have greatly increased offensive forces in Cuba and in Eastern Europe.

- Their fighter aircraft have recently harassed *civilian airliners* in the Berlin air corridor, and they have imposed unilateral and illegal changes on our air traffic to Berlin.

- Throughout 1984, Soviet forces in the Warsaw Pact have been reinforced, and in mid-year a new Soviet Western Front High Command was activated to enhance Warsaw Pact combat readiness.

- Large numbers of Soviet Army reservists (including those assigned to nuclear and chemical missile units) have been recently called up for active service in Eastern Europe.

- The Soviets have withdrawn all military trucks from use in the 1984 grain harvest. The last time they took this unusual step was in 1968, when they invaded Czechoslovakia.

- In 1984, Soviet ammunition factories serving the Warsaw Pact were ordered to begin around the clock operation to produce massive quantities of ammunition for war reserve stockpiles. The order has not been rescinded.

- Soon after Christmas 1984, a Soviet warship fired a nuclear-capable, sea-launched, cruise missile across Norway, then claimed it was a mistake.

Yet the overall recent pattern of increased Soviet intimidation of the United States has in no way been restricted to pressure on NATO.

- Off the United States itself, within minutes of Washington, D.C., on at least *five* occasions in 1984, they have penetrated the U.S. Air Defense Identification Zone with the nuclear-capable TU-95 Bear strategic bomber/reconnaissance aircraft.

- In the Far East, they murdered 61 Americans, including the first member of the U.S. Congress ever known to be assassinated by the Soviets, by shooting down Korean Airlines Flight—007 with 269 innocent people aboard.*

- In Vietnam, in June, 1984, the Soviets added nine TU-16 nuclear bombers to the Soviet reconnaissance aircraft already deployed at Camranh Bay.

- In Japan, on June 18, 1984, the Soviets penetrated Japanese airspace with three Backfire strategic nuclear bombers thus intensifying a practice of frequent violation of Japanese sovereignty including the ongoing occupation of Japanese islands in the southern Kurils and the harrassment of shipping in the strait of Nemuro.

---

*Although rarely explained in the Press, this act occurred over international waters in the Sea of Japan.

- In Afghanistan, they have continued carpet and incendiary bombing and the employment of genocidal warfare techniques including the use of chemical agents against entire villages.

- In the Middle East, they have stationed combat troops in Syria and in Lebanon and have thus backed and emboldened the Syrian and Iranian sponsored terrorists responsible for three Beirut Embassy attacks and the massacre of 241 U.S. Marines.

- In Africa, they have increased Cuban troop strength in Angola to over 40,000 in 15 combat brigades and have provided 1,500 of their own troops to operate heavy weapons while sabotaging negotiations for the independence of Namibia.

- In Central America, during 1984, they sharply escalated arms and munitions shipments to Cuba, Nicaragua, and El Salvador; trained in Bulgaria 40 Nicaraguan MIG pilots; and provided in Cuba advanced MIG aircraft apparently earmarked for the Nicaraguan Air Force. Of special significance, they have completed 8,000 feet of a 12,000 foot military airfield at Punta Huete near the Nicaraguan capital city of Managua and have built two of a planned three military ground control interceptor (GCI) radar stations. When completed, these installations will support Soviet/Cuban strategic airpower in Central America, extend the reach of Soviet strategic bombers to South America, and provide direct super-power military support to the unpopular and dictatorial Nicaraguan Communist elite.

- In further defiance of the United States, the Soviets have also provided Nicaragua with at least 3,500 Cuban troops, over 10,500 Soviet and Warsaw Pact military and security advisors, and a vast quantity of additional war materiels needed to support the planned rapid expansion of the Nicaraguan Army and Militia from a present level of about 200,000 (the largest in Central America) to a force of up to one-half million men which will give the Soviets control of an armed force in Central America approaching the size of the entire regular United States Army worldwide.

- Off North America, in the Bering Sea, in September, 1984, the USSR seized an American ship in international water and impounded it in order to emphasize their unfounded claim to oil under waters purchased from Russia by the United States in 1867. And in on-going territorial negotiations with the USSR, the U.S. Department of State has again collapsed under Soviet pressure and is giving up American claims to Wrangels Island and granting oil concessions to Russia in American waters off Alaska.

- In the USSR itself, during 1984, the Soviets put off limits to American diplomats cities and areas previously open, they dispatched KGB thugs to beat up American diplomats and embassy personnel (including a Marine) on permitted visits to Leningrad,* and they contemptuously spurned our entreaties to free various political prisoners and to comply with the Helsinki Human Rights Agreement.

- They have increased the drumbeat of war propaganda within the USSR and have been more successful than ever in misleading their own people into believing that the United States is preparing an anti-Russian war and that *we* might conceivably attack them at any time.

- In 1984, they practiced the simulated nuclear war evacuation of entire Soviet cities.

- In 1984, their leaders publicly compared President Reagan to Hitler and with no justification (except our protest of *their* invasion of Afghanistan) tried to sabotage the Olympics in Los Angeles.

- They recently deliberately vented outside their own borders nuclear radioactive debris (which reached the U.S.) from an underground nuclear weapons test, an event which is strictly prohibited by the 1963 Limited Test Ban Treaty.

*The attack on the Marine, Sgt. Ronald Campbell of North Island, California, was described by the Department of State as representing a "disturbing *pattern* of official involvement in a campaign to harass and isolate Americans in the Soviet Union." (Compare the non-reaction of our news media in covering these events to their likely response if so much as a finger were laid on any Russian anywhere in our country.)

- They have initiated a major new propaganda campaign against U.S. anti-nuclear space weapons, a disinformation effort which our intelligence community believes may reach the massive proportions of the anti-neutron "bomb" campaign of 1977-1978 which prevented U.S. deployment of enhanced radiation (anti-tank) weapons in Europe (This new KGB campaign had had the *de facto* support of Congress which has prohibited testing of U.S. space weapons. The effort is ancillary to the new Soviet push to dominate space warfare.

- They have initiated a major new propaganda campaign against U.S. anti-nuclear space weapons, a disinformation effort which our intelligence community believes may reach the massive proportions of the anti-neutron "bomb" campaign of 1977-1978 which prevented U.S. deployment of enhanced radiation (anti-tank) weapons in Europe. (This new KGB campaign has had the *de facto* support of Congress which has prohibited testing of U.S. space weapons. The effort is ancillary to the new massive Soviet push to dominate space warfare.)

- In early 1984, they accelerated efforts to develop and produce a horrifying new generation of biological weapons, in spite of international exposure of this activity.

- Throughout 1984, in joint U.S.-USSR sessions of the Standing Consultative Committee on SALT, they have shown complete contempt for our protests of their arms control violations. With increasing openness and with hardly the pretense of excuse, they continue to violate *all* existing arms control treaties. (When they are confronted with a bald faced lie, we can almost hear the tide of bemused and disdainful laughter rolling from Novaya Zemly to the Caucasus. With the power they dispose, *they could care less what we think.)*

- *Simultaneously and without a trace of shame,* while adding *five* nuclear warheads to their own arsenal *each day* (the U.S. is reducing warheads), they have intensified the KGB-linked "nuclear freeze" propaganda campaign aimed at blocking the MX missile, the Trident II missile, or any other program which might begin to rectify the present gross degree of American nuclear inferiority.

All of the foregoing Soviet activities, considered together, are fully consistent with Marshal Ogarkov's call for Soviet national mobilization on a wartime basis. These activities are also ominously consistent with an intention to use new military power for secret political intimidation as well as with the oft repeated Russian subterfuge, a prime feature of Russian history, in which the olive branch of peace is offered publicly to induce a potential victim population to demand its own disarmament.

The picture is too unmistakable to misperceive. The USSR has done all those things that it needs to do in order to be in a position to mobilize swiftly and with surprise its entire strategic potential for the initiation of war. That central fact alone is far more threatening than any single component part, but of the component parts, the potential for nuclear blackmail is the most immediately dangerous to American national independence.

To understand completely how the Soviets are using their awesome military potential for political intimidation, we must recognize that, unlike American forces, Soviet forces are equipped, trained, deployed, and exercised in such a way that they can be used massively and simultaneously on many fronts and at any force level *in first strike attack with very little or no warning.* The significance of this new Soviet posture of high readiness for surprise action, the keystone of Soviet military doctrine, is that Americans are already gradually beginning to behave in ways affected by Soviet desires and some degree of Soviet control.

Even so, on November 5, 1984, in his election eve address to the nation, President Reagan told us that "not one square foot of territory" had been lost to Communism during his Presidency. Literally, he was right. Not one new openly Soviet regime has been established in the last four years. Without denigrating the value of that achievement, we must, however, determine whether what *has occurred instead* is not of equal or greater danger.

With the recent enormous growth of Soviet military potential, there have been fundamental changes in the rules and methods of the protracted conflict. The Cold War measurements of lost or gained territory, of lines in the sand, and of clearly defined pro-Soviet and anti-Soviet governments are no longer either accurate or rational. They have become obsolete through the sheer extent and pervasive effect of Soviet might.

The question then is today not what new geographic territory can be colored red but what degree of Soviet hegemony is being asserted globally. The question is not whether nations have fallen but whether nations are freely ordering their own affairs without reference to Soviet wishes. The question is not whether the United States is strong but whether the Soviet Union is perceived by the world as infinitely stronger and can coerce behavior accordingly.

Confronted with the new overwhelming force backed by the old unstinting aggressive intent, the frontier boundaries have been blurred, the trusted walls rendered useless, the cherished institutions subverted, and all thought of total containment of the foe reduced to a forgotten memory of a bygone era. *The rules have changed.* In the new reality the question is not whether the enemy is within the city walls but whether the oppressive weight of his power without turns our will within to his own.

This concept and process has been understood before. In October, 1938, surveying Nazi use of military intimidation against England during the Munich negotiations, Winston Churchill observed:

> "What I find unendurable is the sense of our country falling into the power, into the orbit and influence of Nazi Germany, and of our existence becoming dependent upon their good will or pleasure."

Surveying Communist use of military intimidation against the United States and against the world, *our response* should be no less intolerant.

CHAPTER V

Awakening

*"The way to victory is long
The going will be hard
We will do the best we can
with what we've got
We must have more planes and
ships—at once
We will win through—
in time"*

Admiral Ernest J. King
Chief of Naval Operations
December, 1941

Admiral King inspired the United States Navy and the American people with the resolution of his words *and his actions* in the desperate days immediately after the Japanese surprise attack on Pearl Harbor. If a surprise attack on America were to come today, there would be time neither for inspiration nor for beginning the process of rebuilding defenses to "win through—in time."

All of America is today as vulnerable to surprise attack as our Pacific Fleet was in 1941 at its distant island outpost. Today, to prevent attack and to avert the subjugation of fear from perpetual vulnerability to attack, we must regain the ability to win the crucial first battle and be prepared, surprised or not, to wage it. And we are now neither prepared to fight nor able to win.

There is, nevertheless, still great value to be found in our time in Admiral King's words of more than four decades ago, because in many ways the unheralded Soviet military growth of the last decade matches in stealth and efficiency the surprise achieved in the Japanese bombing of our fleet. In fact, the USSR has gained in 1985 a degree of *strategic* surprise far more dangerous to our country than the *tactical* surprise we suffered at Pearl Harbor.

For those reasons, we should now particularly heed Admiral King's parallel admonitions to "do the best we can with what we've got" and to get "more planes and ships—at once."

And yes, truly restoring our defenses, in lieu of cosmetic and empty rhetoric, will require firm commitment of spirit, and it will be truly expensive in resources. We will need much more than additional "planes and ships." Very likely, instead of spending one dollar in twenty of the GNP as now, we may need to spend two (as we did in safety in the 1950's and 60's), but that *voluntary* sacrifice, if made, would still nowhere near equal the sacrifice *demanded* of Soviet citizens in their war footing economy.

Then too, in American politics there will always remain the perpetually vexing issue of priorities. How in a "caring society" can we possibly devote more than 17% of government spending to national security? For Americans, the answer ought to be simple: No society can be truly caring unless it is free, and no society is free for long unless its people give preeminence to the protection of liberty in common defense as the first and the overriding duty of government.

Now that we have squandered vast material treasure on failed social welfare programs, we must return to true caring and make collective survival in freedom our first priority and the cornerstone of all other concerns.

Yet how can that goal be secured? A complete answer is beyond the scope of this volume and of the abilities and experience of the authors. Certain general guidelines, however, should be clear to us all.

First, the United States is still a democracy and our destiny is still largely in our own hands.

Second, the government and government leaders are *not* alone responsible for our failures, *we are responsible.**

Third, the government and government leaders must be held fully accountable for failure *by us* as the primary means for discharging our own responsibility.

Fourth, widespread public dissemination of the facts of our present danger is *not* a sufficient answer. We can all be quietly enslaved smugly telling each other how right we were in predicting the event.

Fifth, collective knowledge is much less important than individual acts which, if based in knowledge, will inevitably lead to group action.

Sixth, it is not necessary to have a majority to win; the objective is not therefore 51%, but it *is* the preservation of

---

*This concept of public responsibility (and of the crisis of our inaction) was well expressed by Secretary of Defense Weinberger when he told Congress on February 3, 1985, "the final pledge, *the real commitment,* must be made by the American people ... *that decision must be made this year."*

freedom *for all* regardless what percentage may value the gift or understand the requirements.

Seventh, it *is* necessary to act, to put down the beer and turn off the NFL, to have the guts to be at times unfashionable, to accept sight in the land of the blind, and to move in the world as thus seen rather than to accept the comfort of accepted illusion.

But what action should we individually take? What practical step can we first take? One of our greatest strengths is that the answer to that question is a function of each individual who has the courage to do anything at all.* It is a function of the individual's position in life and society and his corresponding ability to effect change. Some can effect change directly, some can exert pressure at high levels, some can exert pressure at other levels, some can speak publicly, some can give money, some can write letters, some can inquire, and some can answer, but all according to their capability can and must act.

In so doing, it is important to maintain a practical approach and to keep government accountability as a first objective.

The government is charged with providing for the common defense, and we have a duty as citizens to demand efficiency and safety. Here are some practical ways how.

Always separate the crucial from the non-essential.

Most national security decisions made by Congress and the President fall in a gray area where plausible arguments can be made on both sides of the issue. Thus, for example, while a good case can be made that American taxpayer support of the international financial institutions and of imprudent sovereign risk lending by private banks is support beneficial to Soviet objectives, rational arguments can *also* be advanced to the contrary. But *many* other decisions, on the basis of objective fact, can be fairly characterized as having essentially *only two clear sides*: a pro-Soviet position and a pro-American position.

In making this distinction, we do not say that a Congressman voting on the pro-Soviet side is *per se* pro-Soviet in belief, far more likely he simply lacks intellectual capacity sufficient to appreciate the implications of his choice. We do say, how-

---

*It is difficult in this context not to recall the ancient observation of Demosthenes: "Some people think they can stump the man who dares to speak out by asking him what's to be done. To those I will give what I believe is the fairest and truest answer: don't do what you are doing now."

ever, that certain defense questions tested in Congress are so fundamental to American security that ignorance alone can be no excuse. It is on these fundamental and crucial questions that our initial individual actions should therefore focus.

In the past few years, there have arisen several prime examples of that type of basic security issue which we outline now for consideration, not necessarily in order of importance.

The ASAT Decision

The USSR has four types of anti-satellite (ASAT) systems and has had the operational capability to shoot down American satellites *for more than a decade*. This capability has important strategic value because, in the event of war or threat of war, the Soviets could blind our intelligence collecting ability so that we could neither accurately characterize a Soviet attack nor target our own response. The Soviets are upgrading their ASAT systems.

The United States has *no* anti-satellite capability. The United States has attempted to develop an operational low-altitude ASAT using the F-15 fighter aircraft firing a SRAM/ALTAIR Missile. Congress has *prohibited* the testing of this system against a target satellite.

Congressmen voting for these prohibitions supported the Soviet position that there should be a moratorium on U.S. ASAT testing as an initial concession in, and pre-condition for, space weapon negotiations.

From a Soviet perspective, these negotiations would be intended to bring any U.S. ASAT program to a permanent halt, to stymie American anti-nuclear space defenses, and thus to preserve intact the Soviet offensive nuclear advantage without any need to worry over America achieving an effective active defense in space. Many Congressmen apparently either did not understand that perspective or agreed with it.

The Minuteman III Decision

President Carter shut down Minuteman III ICBM production and dismantled the production facility; however, about 100 Minuteman III missiles remain stockpiled in warehouses. The current deployed force consists of 450 Minuteman IIs (obsolete, single warhead) and 550 Minuteman IIIs (obsolescent, three warheads). There are insufficient Minuteman IIs stockpiled for the Minuteman II test program (periodic test firings to maintain confidence that the aging missiles will still work).

In 1981-1982, Congress appropriated $5 million to begin to retrofit 50 stockpiled Minuteman III missiles into 50 Minuteman II silos, the replaced missiles from which would themselves thereafter be stockpiled for testing. This program was thus intended to create a force of 600 Minuteman IIIs, 400 Minuteman IIs, about 50 Minuteman III test missiles and about 50 Minutemen II test missiles—all at a cost less than the price of *one* modern fighter.

But there was a problem: the retrofit program would also have *added* 100 new nuclear warheads with some limited potential for destroying Soviet ICBM silos, and the Soviets were not pleased. Moreover, by 1987, the retrofitted missiles *might* violate SALT which the U.S. steadfastly obeys (even in predicting the future) and Russia relentlessly violates.

The Result: The Air Force spent the initial $5 million bulldozing earth at the missile sites (an action which did not offend the Soviets), and Congress (actually a key staff member of the Senate Subcommittee on Strategic Forces) killed the program in 1983. The staff member was, incidentally, promoted to a position of greater responsibility in the Department of Defense.

The MX Decision

President Carter proposed a new ICBM force of 200 modern MX missiles based on movable launchers so that the missile could be moved and hidden to provide protection against Soviet attack. The new missile was needed because of the Soviet ability to destroy all of our older Minuteman missiles on the ground.

Under Congressional pressure, President Reagan has cut the MX program in half from 200 deployed missiles to a planned 100 and has further provided that these new missiles will *replace* 100 Minuteman IIIs in *vulnerable* silos. Obsolete Minuteman IIs are not to be replaced for reasons apparently related to U.S. compliance with SALT which the USSR is violating.

As a result of the above, the current MX program is of marginal strategic value since the new missiles will be undefended and equally as vulnerable to Soviet attack as the obsolescent replaced Minuteman IIIs. Nevertheless, the new MX missile would have greater accuracy and firepower than our older ICBMs and for that reason alone should be produced.

The Soviet Union, which is developing and fielding *four* new types of ICBMs and has an *existing* operational force using five different types of very modern and large land missiles, *does not want the United States to produce the MX*, which would be the first new American ICBM developed in 17 years.

On October 11, 1984, pending further action, Congress prohibited production of the MX.

The Polaris/Poseidon Decision

During the past few years, in order to comply with SALT while confirming that the Soviets are violating it, the United States has destroyed or deactivated ten perfectly good nuclear-powered Polaris missile submarines by cutting up the missile launchers and pouring concrete in the missile bays.* These submarines had been built at considerable taxpayer cost and could have been converted (consistent with SALT) into Sea Launched Cruise Missile/SLCM) Submarines—as is done in the Soviet Union with *their* older SSBN missile submarines, e.g. the Soviet Yankee Class. However, the Soviets preferred that the *American* submarines simply be destroyed: The dismantled Polaris force is now awaiting environmental approval to be sunk at sea or buried in the land.

In the defense budget for fiscal year 1985 are 21 million dollars to begin the destruction of the even newer Poseidon missile submarine force. Since the Environmental Protection Agency makes it expensive to destroy a perfectly good nuclear submarine, these funds are probably sufficient to begin cutting up only two Poseidon missile boats. But eventually six Poseidon submarines, at the insistence of the Department of State, *must* be destroyed to comply with SALT which the Soviets are violating.

These latest, very expensive nuclear submarines, *which are being readied today for destruction,* carry the Trident I SLBM (the C-4 SLBM) which is our newest submarine launched missile. Although the Trident I is greatly inferior to modern

*Two of the Polaris boats were converted into special operations attack submarines. Three others have been deactivated but not yet destroyed.

118

Soviet SLBMs, the USSR would prefer that the Trident Is on the Poseidons be removed permanently as a deterrent threat to the Soviet Union.

Congress, in October, 1984, voted taxpayer funding to grant that wish.

The Trident II Decision

For a number of years, the United States has been developing the Trident II SLBM (the D-5) which would be a long-range submarine missile comparable to existing modern Soviet SLBMs. The new missile, because of its greater range, would increase the patrol area of its submarine so that the sub would be harder for the Soviets to find. Additionally, the missile could be made accurate enough to knock out Soviet ICBM silos and thus help to protect America from nuclear weapons as opposed simply to threatening the Russian people with our nuclear weapons.

For those reasons, the USSR does not like the U.S. Trident II program.

Moreover, the original idea was that the Trident II would be deployed in the large missile wells of the new Trident submarines. But this plan also conflicted with Soviet wishes.

At present, the new large Trident submarines are armed with the small Trident I SLBM (again the C-4) which about one-half fills the Trident missile well and coincidentally is the same missile carried in the Poseidon boats slated for destruction.

The reason for these anomalies: a series of Congressional and Administration actions which have delayed production of the Trident II SLBM (the D-5) until after 1990 even though the missile could have been ready for operation by 1985 or 1986.

But even so, the Trident II's status is not yet fully decided. By 1990 there is every likelihood that the Soviets will again get their way, and, as in the case of the MX, Congress will block or delay funds for Trident II deployment production.

The Binary Chemical Weapons Decision

The Soviet Union has massive stockpiles of modern chemical weapons. The United States has no modern chemical weapons.

The U.S. binary chemical weapon program was initiated in order to give our country a limited number of safe-to-handle chemical weapons to match at least fractionally the Soviet stockpile. These proposed binary weapons would have *no* toxic potential whatsoever until the two parts of the weapon are combined immediately prior to use in combat.

The Soviet Union did not wish the United States to have binary chemical munitions and thus a chemical deterrent. Instead, it wished very much to retain its monopoly of modern chemical weapons and the undeterred advantage conferred by its enormous stockpile.

Congress, in 1983, prohibited production of U.S. binary chemical munitions.

Summary

Decisions of the type described above—and there are many more—are not in our view evidence of treason but neither are they in the gray area of national security questions about which reasonable men can disagree. They are clear cut. In each case cited, one position favors the USSR and its opposite favors America.

It is on these clear-cut questions, therefore, that each individual should act. The gray areas can wait. We have limited time, numbers, and energy; so those who believe action is required must concentrate their effort where it can have the greatest and earliest effect.

Permit us therefore one final recommendation . . . based on twelve years of combined observation in staffing Congress—do *not* write your Congressman.

 Do not write your Senators and Representatives about defense issues of the foregoing magnitude. The Congressman would likely *not* see your letter and his written response would likely be prepared by a youthful staff member who would have little idea what you are talking about and even less interest in finding out.

 Do contact your Senators and Representatives *on the telephone*** or meet with them in person: Try not to accept an aide as a substitute, and if *your man* refuses to talk with you di-

---

*Senators or Congressmen can be reached by calling the Capitol switchboard at (202) 224-3121 and asking for the Senator or Representative by name.

rectly, consider writing your local newspaper to complain of his inaccessability.

Do not, however, become a nuisance. Ask the Congressman to do no more than one thing at a time, and when he responds properly, thank him profusely and consider helping his campaign. But when he does wrong (or even looks as if he might)—especially on a fundamental security question in which he appears disposed to act as the Soviet Union would wish—*sink your teeth in his neck like a bulldog and hang on.*

Remember: the United States belongs to us all—not just to the ill-informed men and women who all too often make up the bewildered majority in Washington.

Never be bashful. Act now, and act again and again. The informed and result-oriented Congressmen (there are many) desperately need the support of your help, and the remainder—the lost and wandering—are there to hear you and your judgments and to be given direction and purpose.

We owe our Senators and Representatives always the sincere respect due their high office, and we owe some Senators and Representatives deep personal respect for their actions, but we also owe each of them, one and all, the benefit of our ideas when we are sure they are soundly based in fact. If we do not discharge that last obligation to our Representatives in Washington, and to our fellow citizens, as best we are able, then we individually will have no grounds for complaint should the day of our national awakening come too late for our wonderful country, ourselves, and our families and for freedom.

EPILOGUE

Choices

"If we lose our faith in ourselves, in our capacity to guide and govern, if we lose our will to live, then indeed our story is told."

Churchill, 1933

In this book we have painted a grim yet truthful picture. We have given to the best of our ability an accurate, current assessment of the decline of American military strength and of the ascendance of Soviet military power and its implications.

What we cannot assess and have not attempted to gauge is the American spirit, whether enough Americans will care enough about freedom to resist the new tyranny and its promise of eventual enslavement. That answer is locked in each American's heart throughout our homeland.

We believe that the story of the American Republic is far from over, but we are also convinced that the text of what may prove the final chapter is already written and waits only on time to be told.

If our course does not change and history with it, in that last day, Americans could face an awesome decision: whether to risk the liberty and life of our Republic through almost inevitable defeat in a desperate, withering, and pointless war or whether to accept an even worse end—through tacit surrender and gradual subjugation to overwhelming totalitarian power.

Those alternatives must be avoided, but each day of our inaction makes it more difficult to turn away as we beguile our friends, our families, and ourselves in the belief that all is well. And yet, our whole history as a people impels us to act, to face the unhappy truth of our worsening condition and to choose the hard task of survival in freedom.

Many, if not most Americans will avoid the rigor of looking the enemy in the eye and seeing his strength; many if not most Americans will no doubt continue to avert their gaze and prefer the ease and the torpor and the comfort of denying history, of denying that republics do fall, of denying the new potential for a lingering national death. But so was the case before when American liberty was threatened—and yet a very few who were imbued with lust for freedom prevailed against

123

both a tyrant king and the indolence of their own countrymen. In that day as in this, the test was not so much of strength as it was of will.

Ironically, in writing this book we have drawn heavily on the inspired wisdom and determined courage of Winston Churchill, a descendant of those same oppressors of our early national life. We have done so because of his foresight, because of his clarity of thought and vigor of expression, because of the remarkable, prescient applicability of his long-ago words to our time and condition today, but chiefly because of his overarching love of liberty.

Therefore it is worth remembering that the Americans for whom this book is written share with Churchill at least one great honor, given to us by birth and to him by Act of Congress—American Citizenship. Also worth remembering from this our adopted countryman are a final warning and a hard choice.

The warning was given in 1935:

"The lessons of history are part of that long dismal catalogue of the fruitlessness of experience, and the confirmed unteachability of mankind. Want of foresight, unwillingness to act when action would be simple and effective, lack of clear thinking, confusion of counsel until the emergency comes, until self-preservation strikes its jarring gong, these are the features which constitute the endless repetition of history."

The choice was made in 1939:

"War is horrible, but slavery is worse."

We who desire life in both liberty *and* peace must heed in time the warning; otherwise we too, in time, will surely face the choice.

*Compendium of Official Charts
Prepared by the U.S. Government
Depicting Soviet Military
Superiority*

ICBM REENTRY VEHICLES — WARHEADS (U)

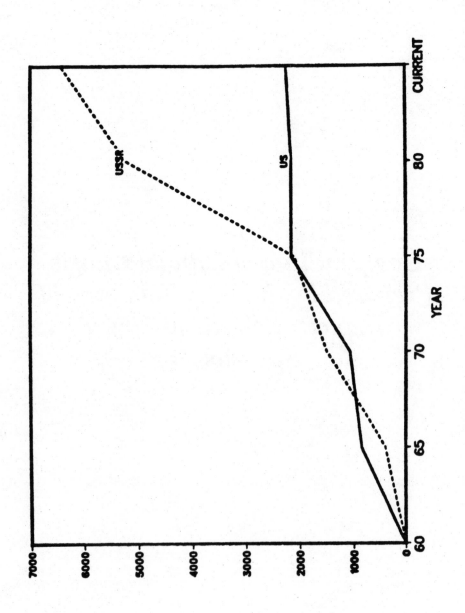

BALLISTIC MISSILE SUBMARINES (U)

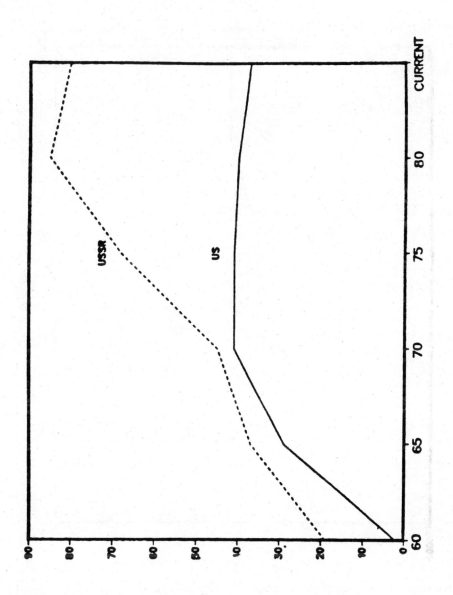

SUBMARINE LAUNCHED BALLISTIC MISSILE LAUNCHERS (U)

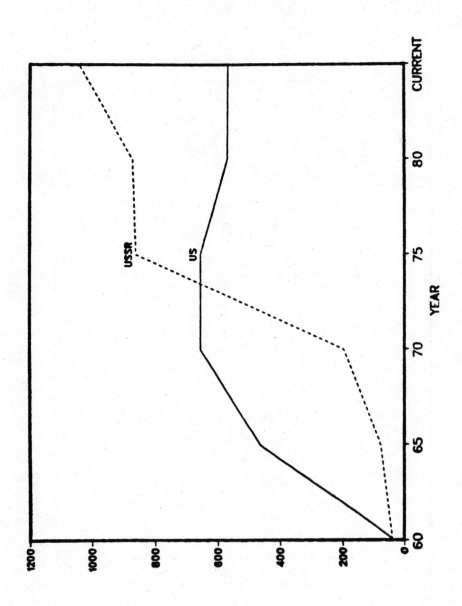

INTERCONTINENTAL SUPERSONIC BOMBERS (U)

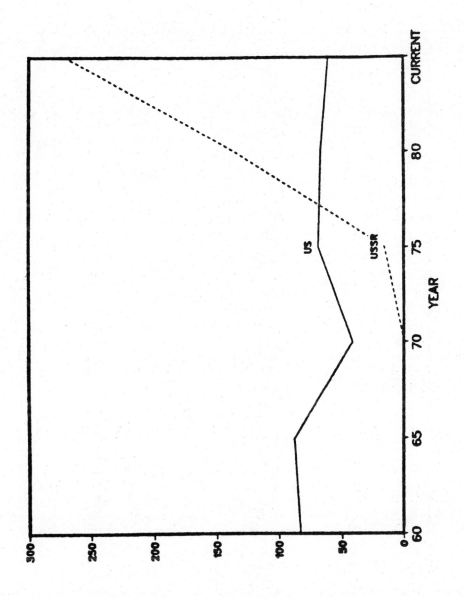

LONG RANGE INF WARHEADS (U)

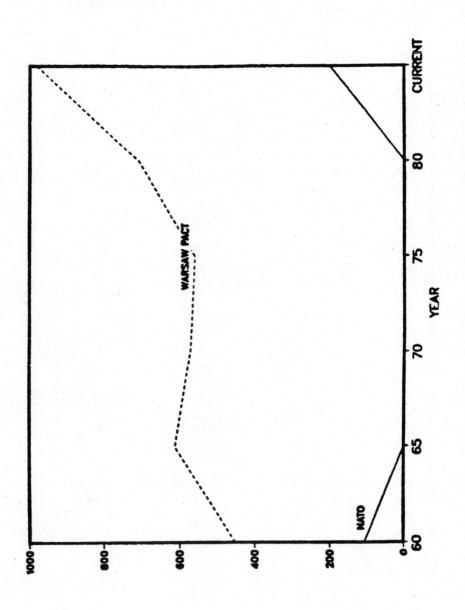

SUPERSONIC INTERCEPTOR AIRCRAFT (U)

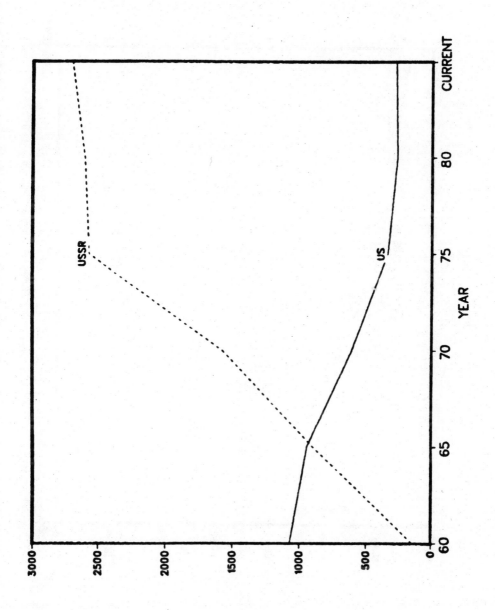

SURFACE TO AIR MISSILE LAUNCHERS (U)

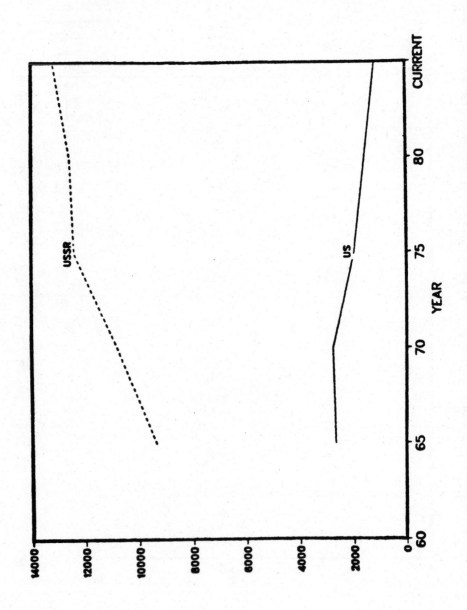

TACTICAL COMBAT AIRCRAFT (U)

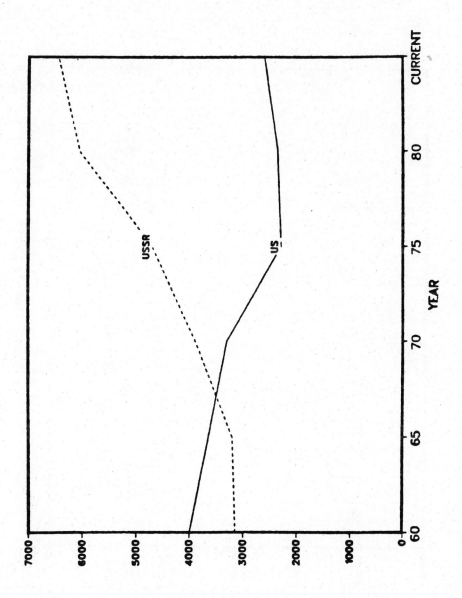

TANKS (U)

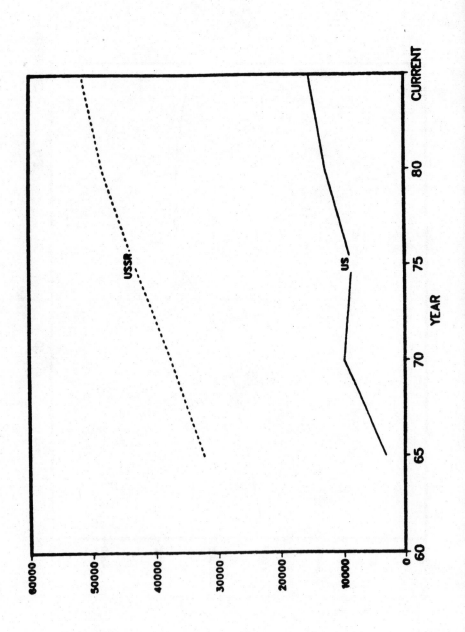

OTHER ARMORED VEHICLES (U)

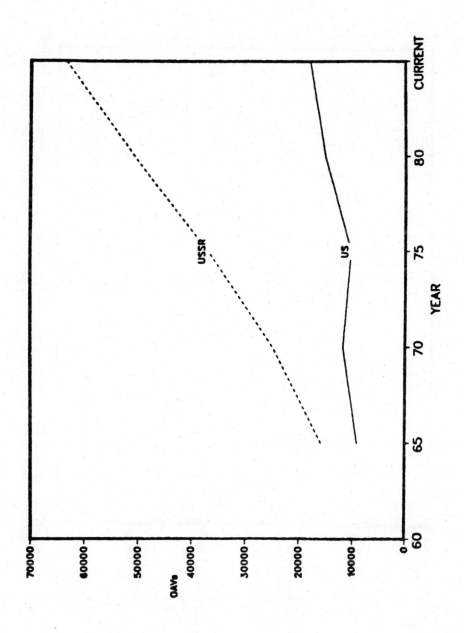

ARTILLERY (U)

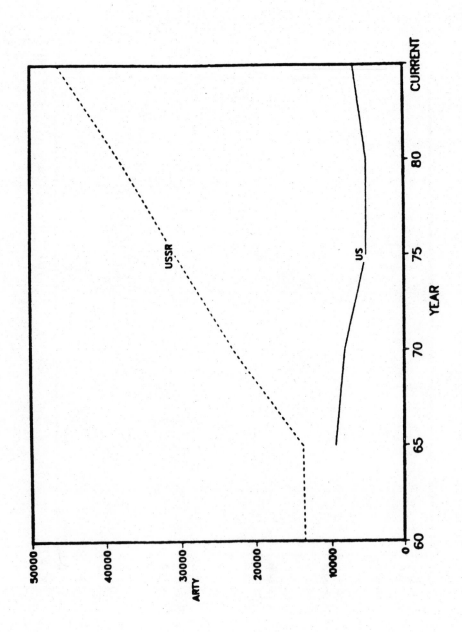

APPENDIX II

Representative Description of Soviet Arms Control Violations

"Inter Arma Silent Legis"

Roman Maxim

In April, 1984, the Department of Defense stated in *Soviet Military Power*:

"To the Soviets, treaties are manipulated in the manner most conducive to the interests of national policy objectives."

This assessment is borne out in an analysis of Soviet treaty compliance behavior since 1917 and in this fundamental Soviet directive issued *in* 1917 upon the founding of the USSR:

"Deception is an arrangement of light and dark . . . the people must be made to see white where there is black."

Sixty-seven years later, President Reagan stated in his *Report to the Congress on Soviet Non-Compliance with Arms Control Agreements,* dated January 23, 1984, that:

"The United States Government has determined that the Soviet Union is violating:

1. The Geneva Protocol on Chemical Weapons,
2. The Biological Weapons Convention,
3. The Helsinki Final Act,
4. telemetry encryption and
5. a rule concerning ICBM modernization.

"In addition we have determined that the Soviet Union:

6. has almost certainly violated the ABM Treaty (SALT I),
7. probably violated the SALT II limit on new types (of ICBMs)
8. probably violated the SS-16 deployment prohibition of SALT II,
9. and is likely to have violated the nuclear testing yield limit of the Threshold Test Ban Treaty."

In a related comment, the Department of Defense has asserted:

"Several of these violations must have been planned by Soviet authorities many years ago, in some cases perhaps *at the very time the Soviet Union entered into the agreements.*"

Unfortunately, however, the President's January, 1984 Report on Soviet SALT violations covers only the tip of the iceberg on Soviet arms control treaty breach. This appendix will therefore attempt to outline some of the other examples of Soviet cheating.

In so doing we bear in mind that, according to the official 1962 Defense Department book, *Soviet Treaty Violations*, there have been over 50 fundamental Soviet breaches of international security and non-agression treaties since 1917.

Here are a few:

Case I

In a letter to Congress dated April 19, 1984, the U.S. Arms Control and Disarmament Agency officially confirmed that the Soviet Union had repeatedly violated the 1963 Limited Test Ban Treaty by "numerous Soviet ventings involving dispersal of radioactive materials beyond Soviet borders."

Case II

On September 14, 1983, President Reagan for a second time confirmed that the Soviet Union had violated the 1962 Kennedy-Khrushchev Agreement which ended the Cuban Missile Crisis:

"... that agreement has been abrogated many times by the Soviet Union and Cuba in the bringing of what can only be considered offensive weapons, not defensive, there."

Case III

The President's General Advisory Committee (GAC) on Arms Control confirmed the following new violations in a report to Congress on October 10, 1984:

1. The Nuclear Test Moratorium, 1958-1961
2. The Kennedy-Khrushchev Agreement of 1962.
3. The Limited Test Ban Treaty of 1963.
4. The Montreaux Convention of 1936
5. The SALT I Interim Agreement and the ABM Treaty of 1972 involving widespread camouflage, concealment, cover and deception.
6. The SALT I Interim Agreement of 1972 involving excess ballistic missile launchers.
7. The SALT I ABM Treaty involving the ABM-3 movable ABM radar currently in mass production and deployment.
8. The 1981 Conventional Weapons Convention in Afghanistan.
9. The 1982 Brezhnev Moratorium on SS-20 Deployment.
10. The unratified SALT II Treaty of 1979 involving their massive increase in strategic camouflage, concealment, and deception.
11. The 1972 SALT I Interim Agreement through deployment of their medium SS-17 ICBM and their *heavy* SS-19 ICBM to replace illegally their light SS-11 ICBM.
12. Tests of surface to air missiles and radars in a prohibited ABM mode in violation of the SALT I ABM Treaty.

Case IV
Further Soviet SALT Violations

1. Production of 35 Backfire bombers per year, in violation of SALT II commitments. Arctic staging of the Backfire,

giving Backfire an intercontinental refueling capability, and deceiving the United States with respect to its 8,900-11,000 kilometer range and ALCM capability.

2. Deployment of the Soviet SS-NX-23 heavy SLBM, in violation of SALT II.

3. Soviet violation of the 820, 1,200, 1,320 MIRV/ALCM, SALT II ceilings, and exceeding the 2,250 SALT II ceilings on strategic nuclear delivery vehicles by over 550 delivery vehicles.

4. Developing and testing the Soviet SS-18 ICBM rapid reload/refire capability and reported SS-18 tests circumventing SALT II MIRV ceilings.

5. The Soviet testing of an ABM rapid reload and refire capability prohibited by SALT I.

6. The Soviet preparations for deployment of a nationwide ABM defense involving ABM Battle Management Radars, plus ABM-mode mobile SAM interceptors and ABM-3 mobile radars.

7. Keeping 18 SS-9 ICBMs operational at a test range in circumvention of SALT I.

8. Violating the Brezhnev SALT I pledge not to build mobile ICBMs.

9. Deploying SS-11s at MRBM and IRBM soft sites for covert soft launch in circumvention of SALT II ceilings.

10. Maintaining several thousand stockpiled ICBMs, SLBMs, and SCMs, and thus circumventing all SALT II ceilings.

11. Increasing Soviet use of large scale strategic camouflage, concealment, and deception, including *jamming* of U.S. telemetry collection satellites.

12. Deploying 14 warheads on SS-18s, when SALT II allows only 10.*

13. Creation of a new ABM test range without prior notification in violation of the ABM Treaty.

14. Constructing the Stretch Y-Class submarine with a prohibited type of long range SLCM launchers.

15. The blatant Soviet failure to deactivate over 550 strategic delivery vehicles to come down to the agreed SALT II level of 2,250 strategic nuclear delivery vehicles, a breach they openly acknowledge.

*This prohibited increase in warheads is not fully confirmed, but is highly probable.

Case V
Soviet Violations and Circumventions
of the 1972 SALT I Interim Agreement
on Offensive Weapons

1. Deployment of heavy SS-19 ICBM as the replacement for light SS-11.
2. Failure to deactivate old ICBMs on time, continuous falsification of official deactivation reports.
3. Bringing back ICBM equipment to allegedly deactivated ICBM complexes.
4. Keeping 18 SS-9 ICBMs at an ICBM test range illegally operational.
5. Constructing III-X silos with a configuration similar to missile launch silos.
6. Increased use of deliberate camouflage, concealment, and deception by:
   —encryption of missile telemetry
   —camouflage of ICBM testing, production and deployment
   —concealment of SLBM submarine construction, use of dummy subs, and construction of berthing tunnels.
7. Construction of over 68 strategic submarines, when only 62 were allowed.
8. Violation of the Brezhnev pledge not to build mobile ICBMs.
9. Deploying SS-11 ICBMs at SS-4 MRBM soft sites.
10. Keeping 1,300 to several thousand old ICBMs stockpiled for both covert soft launch and rapid reload of silos for refire.

Case VI
Soviet Violations and Circumventions of the
SALT I ABM Treaty

1. Soviet SAM testing in ABM mode—SAM-5, SAM-10, SAM-12.
2. Deployment of 6 or more ABM Battle Management Radars.
3. Deployment of one ABM Battle Management Radar in the interior USSR not facing outward (at Krasnoyarsk)

which also is a potential ICBM defense system.
4. ABM camouflage and concealment.
5. Falsification of ABM deactivation.
6. Building new ABM test range without prior notification.
7. Development and deployment of a movable or mobile ABM-3 radar.
8. Testing of rapid refire ABMs, within two and a half hours.
9. Deployment of nationwide ABM defense—over 20 large radars.
10. Deployment of more than 100 ABM launchers around Moscow.

Case VII
Additional Soviet Violations of the 1979 SALT II Treaty

1. SS-18 rapid reload/refire capability, within 24 hours.
2. Covert deployment of up to 200 SS-16s at the Plesetsk Test Range.
3. AS-3 Kangaro Long Range ALCMs on Bear bombers and building more new Bears.
4. Deployment of long range ALCMs on Backfire bombers, 35 per year, Arctic deployment of Backfires, concealment of their 8,900-11,000 kilometer range and refueling capability.
5. Total (95-100%) encryption of telemetry in testing the following missiles:

ICBM	SLCM	SLBM	IRBM/ICBM
SS-18	SS-N-19	SS-N-20	SS-20
SS-X-24			
SS-X-25			

6. Four new type ICBMs in development or deployment, of which three are prohibited:
SS-24, SS-25, SS-X-26, and SS-X-27
7. The SS-25 Reentry Vehicle (RV) to Throw-weight ratio exceeds limits.
8. Increased large scale strategic camouflage, concealment, and deception.

9. Fourteen warheads on SS-18s, possibly producing up to 1,304 additional prohibited RVs.
10. A new heavy SLBM, the SS-NX-23.
11. Soviet *admission* of the intention to exceed the 820 and 1,200 MIRV limits.
12. Soviet failure to reduce SNDVs to the initial 2,400 and the subsequent 2,250 ceilings.
13. Soviet expansion of forces beyond 2,750 SNDVs-Bear H, Blackjack, Backfire, SS-16, SS-25 road mobile, SS-24 rail mobile, SS-X-26, and SS-X-27.

Case VIII
Negotiating Deceptions

1. SS-16 withheld by Soviets from SALT II Data Base.
2. AS-3 withheld by Soviets from SALT II Data Base.
3. Backfire range and refueling misrepresented, SALT II.
4. SS-19 existence concealed, SALT I.
5. Soviets lied on "Stretch Yankee" submarine, SALT I.
6. Soviets falsified ICBM deactivation reports, SALT I.
7. Soviets concealed SS-N-8 SLBM range, SALT I.
8. Soviets lied on Mutual Balanced Force Reduction (MBFR) troop data.

Case IX
Accidental Release of Anthrax from Biological Warfare Facility at Sverdlovsk

In April, 1979, an accidental Soviet Biological Warfare explosion occurred at Sverdlovsk. More than 1,000 Soviet citizens died from a strain of pulmonary anthrax developed for use in combat. The accident showed that the Soviets had an offensive military capability for biological warfare, which is banned by the 1975 Biological Warfare Convention. The Sverdlovsk accident occurred just one month before the June, 1979 Vienna Summit where the SALT II Treaty was signed.

The Pattern of Soviet Violations

President Reagan, on September 2, 1983, asked these rhetorical questions after the Soviet attack on Korean airlines Flight 007:

> "What can be said about Soviet credibility when they so flagrantly lie...? *What can be the scope of legitimate mutual discourse with a state whose values permit such atrocities?* And what are we to think of a regime which establishes one set of standards for itself and another for the rest of mankind?"

Modern diplomatic history demonstrates that totalitarian nations have systematically circumvented and violated arms control agreements when it served their interests. Specifically, long before SALT began in 1969, the Soviets violated two significant arms control treaties—one in the 1920's, which entailed on-site inspection, and another in the late 1940's. We were aware of that history, yet elected to proceed in good faith and credited the Soviets with similar values. We were mistaken.

As Soviet authorities in international law have stated:

> "Those institutions of international law which can facilitate the accomplishment of the stated tasks of Soviet foreign policy are recognized and applied in the USSR; *those which contradict these aims in any way are rejected.* (F. I. Kozhevnikov, *The Soviet State and International Law*, Moscow, 1948, p. 25.)

But there are still those in the U.S. government who would choose to believe instead the official Soviet propaganda publication entitled *Whence the Threat to Peace* (published in 1982) which denies the existence of any Soviet arms control treaty violations. This Soviet publication states:

> "The Soviet Union's attitude to its international commitments is clearly formulated in the Constitution of the USSR. The Soviet Union has *never* violated the standards of international law or any treaties or agreements. *It has always been a reliable partner in international affairs. 'If we put our signature on a treaty,'* Leonid Brezhnev pointed out, *'We mean that we are fully resolved to adhere to its letter and spirit strictly and entirely."*

These protestations are, of course, ridiculous on their face.

According to an official U.S. State Department *Soviet Affairs Note* dated as long ago as August 10, 1959:

"Few nations can match the USSR in vociferous protestations of loyalty to international obligations. However, such declarations which are typical of Soviet propagandists and scholars alike—diverge widely from Soviet practice. In the years since the Bolshevik Revolution the Soviet government, while consistently accusing others of bad faith in international dealings, has not hesitated to violate its own treaty obligations when such action appeared to be in its interest."

This conclusion is well illustrated by V. I. Lenin's cold admission in 1918 regarding the March, 1918 Soviet/German peace treaty of Brest-Litovsk:

"Yes, of course we are violating the treaty. We have already violated it 30 or 40 times."

The official 1959 State Department analysis of Soviet treaty compliance authoritatively concluded:

"The history of the last 40 years provides numerous examples of deliberate treaty violation by the Soviet regime ... The USSR has disregarded treaty provisions inconvenient to itself, has unilaterally denounced conventions to which it is a party, *has threatened abrogation as a means of intimidation*, and has on several occasions attacked fellow signators to treaties of friendship and non-aggression."

It is evident that the Soviet Union places no value in abiding by international agreements. The Soviet view is that, if an international obligation no longer serves its purposes, Moscow has, and should have, no inhibitions about violating it.

As the record of history indicates, the Soviet approach to its international commitments should warn us that we must create a clear Soviet self-interest in treaty compliance; otherwise, treaties with the Soviets are self-deceptive scraps of paper, which are worse than worthless. In fact, treaties with the USSR can be a positive danger if they lull us into a false sense of security ... as they have done so often in the past.

That same false sense of security has permitted the enormous momentum of the Soviet strategic weapons build-up, which started even before the Cuban Missile Crisis of 1962,* and which will continue into the 1990's . . . unconstrained by existing strategic arms limitations treaties which the U.S. still sanctimoniously observes.

Former Reagan Administration Arms Control Director Eugene Rostow has written:

"The SALT I Agreements and the process of negotiating SALT II did not prevent the worst decade of the Cold War or the extraordinary buildup of the Soviet nuclear arsenal."

A top Reagan Defense official, Dr. Richard DeLauer, told Congress:

"The Soviets in fact never slowed or even perturbed their strategic development and deployment programs in spite of detente, active arms control negotiations, or the SALT agreements."

To which Assistant Secretary of Defense Richard Perle has added that there has been a 75% increase in Soviet nuclear warheads aimed at the United States since SALT II was signed in 1979.

A friend of President Reagan, Laurence Beilenson, summed it up in this fashion in his recent book:

"We consider ourselves sagacious in staking our survival on treaties with the USSR, whose ideology blesses cheating as a virtue." (*Survival and Peace in the Nuclear Age*, Laurence W. Beilenson, Regnery-Gateway, Chicago, 1980, p. 62.)

But the best summation was given by V. I. Lenin himself in 1918:

"Promises are like pie crusts, made to be broken."

---

*Some individuals still erroneously believe that the Soviet nuclear buildup was begun in response to the Cuban Missile Crisis. In fact, the buildup was initiated long before the Crisis, which was *a part of the buildup* rather than a cause for it.

And Lenin's approach has been confirmed as the consistent Soviet approach by official U.S. government documentation that supports the final and inescapable conclusion that the Soviets have violated, evaded, or circumvented virtually every international treaty they have signed since 1917.

But the USSR violates not only its international agreements, it also violates far more basic notions of international conduct.

There is thus strong evidence that the Soviet leadership planned and ordered implemented the plot to assassinate Pope John Paul II in June, 1981. Additionally, Soviet violations of the chemical and biological warfare treaties are more than simple arms control treaty violations. They are intentional atrocities. Thousands of innocent men, women, and children in Southeast and Southwest Asia have died horribly cruel deaths at Soviet hands. And these more recent examples are only a small part of the evidence of history which shows that the Soviet Union is truly an outlaw nation operating at the outer bounds of despotism.

Yet, undeterred by mounds of bodies, by nations enslaved, and by deception after deception after deception, the United States of America continues to negotiate, to negotiate, and to negotiate.

—"Concern and Restraint"—A State Department Drafted Letter Describing How America Is Complying with Arms Agreements Despite Repeated And Continuing Soviet Non-Compliance

The White House
August 6, 1984

Dear [Senator]:

This is in reply to your letters to me of July 2 and July 25, expressing *concern* about this Administration's policy of not undercutting the provisions of SALT II.

It is incorrect to say, as your letter states, that this Administration has turned SALT II into a mutually binding secret executive agreement with the Soviet Union. We have neither negotiated nor signed a secret agreement. What we have done is to adopt a policy of refraining from actions which would undercut SALT II so long as the Soviet Union shows equal *restraint*.

I have stated on many occasions that SALT II did not provide a sound basis for arms control and that a new treaty was necessary. On May 31, 1982, I publicly enunciated our no-undercut policy at the same time that I announced the beginning of the START negotiations. The confidential diplomatic exchanges referred to in the annex to your letter have been carried out solely for the purpose of informing the leaders of the Soviet Union of our policy and seeking an understanding of their policy with regard to SALT II. Nothing has been said to the Soviet Union that goes beyond this policy.

Since the Administration made clear that it did not intend to seek ratification of the SALT II Treaty, there has remained no legal obligation on either party to refrain from acts which would defeat the object and purpose of the agreement. Thus our policy statement with respect to SALT II represents a political commitment rather than a legal obligation. As such, SALT II is not an executive agreement and carries no legal obligations.

The intent of our policy has been to promote an atmosphere of mutual *restraint* which is conducive to strategic nuclear arms negotiations while not jeopardizing U.S. national security. This policy is compatible both with our START objectives and our defense modernization program.

Your letter takes note of the significant *concerns* that have arisen in recent years about Soviet adherence to a comparable policy of *restraint*. I indicated in my January 23, 1984, report to the Congress that we have determined that the USSR has violated or probably violated several provisions of existing arms control accords—both those which are in force, and those to which the Soviet Union claims to be adhering as a matter of policy (as you note in your letter, the Soviets do not claim to be reducing to the 2400/2250 SNDV limits in SALT II). Additional studies of Soviet compliance behavior are in progress. Concurrently, we are endeavoring through diplomatic channels to resolve with the Soviet our *concerns* about such behavior and are seeking explanations, clarifications, and corrective actions. We have stressed that if we are to retain confidence in the continuing utility of our arms control agreements, compliance must be rigorous.

We have made clear to the leaders of the Soviet Union our unequivocal preference for an environment characterized by *mutual restraint* pending the accomplishment of significant mutual and effectively verifiable reductions in destabilizing nuclear systems. We believe this is in our national security interest as well as theirs.

While we strive to realize this goal, however, we are continuing our policy of pursuing needed strategic force modernization while preserving all necessary options to ensure flexibility in our defense programs. This includes the steps, to which you referred, related to the deployment in the fall of 1985 of the seventh Trident submarine. We believe that if we are to succeed in accomplishing these objectives, full funding by the Congress of our defense modernization program is essential.

I hope this explanation of our policy is helpful. As I noted in my report to the Congress last January, the Executive and Legislative branches of our government have long had a shared interest in the arms control process. Finding effective ways to ensure compliance is central to that process. Continued Congressional understanding and support for our approach to arms control is essential.

Sincerely,
[signed] Ronald Reagan

The Honorable John P. East
United States Senate
Washington, D.C. 20510

The Price of Coffee Pots and Bolts

During the past several years, the news media, in what some believe is a calculated attempt to influence the public against *necessary* defense spending, have made a very great clamor about the apparent high price of small components in large military systems. Hardly a day passes without "news" of some new "outrage" wherein the Department of Defense is laid open unmercifully for paying hundreds of dollars per copy for nuts, bolts, screwdrivers, or coffee pots.

Rarely is it explained to the public (which is by now understandably enraged but enraged unjustifiably) that these price anomalies with very few exceptions solely arise from accounting allocations unrelated to actual pricing or, in some other cases, from very limited procurements of "nuts and bolts" made from special materials honed to required technological tolerences.

One unusual acknowledgment of these unstated facts appeared in the *Washington Post* of February 3, 1985, in a column by George Will. Mr. Will's well taken arguments are repeated here because they in this instance are unlikely to be reproduced often anywhere else:

"Pentagon acquisition rules stipulate that 'overhead' expenses be allocated to each shipment at some fixed proportion of the value of the product. If the value is $5 million, the corporation might be entitled to add, say, 20 percent ($1 million) for overhead. Overhead includes costs above materials, machines and labor—costs of everything from legal departments to company headquarters.

"The Pentagon orders many kinds of parts simultaneously. As an approved accounting convenience, many contractors allocate overhead on an "item" rather than "value" basis. . . . an example of [this procedure is] a $20

153

million order for 10,000 parts, some of which have a direct cost of $25,000 each and others of 4 cents each.

"Instead of apportioning the $1 million total overhead such that the $25,000 part gets a lot and the 4-cent part a little, the computer printout will allocate $100 to each part. This produces a charge to the government of $25,100 for the expensive part and $100.04 for the cheap one."

Unfortunately, arcane accounting procedures are of far less interest to anti-defense journalists and their biased editors than the ready-made hype of a $100 screw driver and its effect in creating public ill-will against necessary defense spending.

APPENDIX V

Third Country Strategic Power

—The United Kingdom, France, Communist China, and India—

The United States and the USSR are not the only nations in the world to possess nuclear weapons. Great Britain, France, Communist China, and India are also nuclear powers.

However, the strategic anti-nuclear defenses of the USSR and the awesome offensive nuclear fire power of the Soviets make the nuclear forces of these lesser powers, as compared to Russia, essentially insignificant. Additionally, since these third-nation nuclear forces are not under American control, it would be a grave error to count them glibly on our side of the strategic equation.

Nevertheless, the following is a brief description of the forces involved and an analysis of their potential use.

The United Kingdom

Great Britain possesses no land-based nuclear ballistic missiles. The Royal Navy does, however, operate four Polaris Submarines carrying sixty-four warheads. Some of these weapons could be used to support NATO if the one submarine normally on patrol was not destroyed in a Soviet first strike.

Great Britain also possesses about 40 nuclear delivery capable Vulcan bombers, but these aircraft were built in the 1950's, are obsolete, and could not penetrate Soviet defenses. They no longer have strategic missions.

On October 3, 1984, at its national convention in Blackpool, the British Labor Party (which could easily gain office in the next U.K. general elections) voted *four to one* to adopt a policy of *total* unilateral nuclear disarmament and to banish *all* U.S. atomic weapons from British soil. This new position highlights the imprudence of placing undue confidence in third country nuclear forces (or in *plans* for their future modernization), even in the c se of our closest ally.

France

In 1964, France withdrew from NATO. Therefore, French nuclear weapons are not available even to the North Atlantic Alliance much less to assist the United States.

French strategic forces include 18 Intermediate Range Ballistic Missiles (IRBMs) with 18 warheads, four missile submarines carrying sixty-four warheads, and forty Mirage bombers with no penetration capability against the Soviet Union.

Communist China

The highly-placed Russian KGB defector Anatoliy Golitsin in his book *New Lies For Old* asserts that the postulated Chinese Communist-Russian Communist split is a strategic deception intended to cause the U.S. to rely on an unreliable ally. Golitsin advises that this form of deception is known within the KGB as "the scissors strategy" where the victim is cut in half by what he perceives to be opposing sides.

Whether or not Communist China would, in fact, turn on America in a showdown (as predicted in Allen Drury's *Hill of Summer*) is of less significance than the fact that Red China has only a limited strategic potential against the USSR, whereas it *is* developing strategic potential against the United States.

Communist China tested its first atomic bomb on October 11, 1964,* and its first hydrogen bomb on June 17, 1967, yet Chinese bombers could not in anyone's wildest imagination penetrate *Soviet* air defenses. The Chinese do have in operation at least one ballistic missile submarine, but it has far greater terror potential against an America with no strategic defenses than against a USSR with a growing capability to down SLBMs.

Similarly, the few medium range Chinese CSS-2 and CSS-3 ballistic missiles (there are a total of about 120 deployed) are a much greater threat to non-nuclear equipped U.S. allies in the Pacific (where these Chinese weapons constrained even

---

*This initial nuclear test was heavily supported by previously supplied Soviet technological assistance and coincided with President Lyndon Johnson's nuclear scare campaign against the Republican nominee, Senator Barry Goldwater.

our actions in Vietnam) than they could ever be against Moscow and its *defended* nuclear arsenal. Not only would these missiles have difficulting penetrating Soviet defenses, any launch of the relatively puny Chinese force against the USSR would invite self annihilation.

Of far greater concern to the United States should be the new Chinese CSS-4 ICBM. This new missile can be launched from China and hit Kansas City with a nuclear weapon. Since the CSS-3 missiles can *already* reach Moscow, it should be clear for whom the *new* longer range ICBM is intended. And, unlike the Russians, *we have no ABM defense.*

Finally, uninformed but well-meaning Americans often make much of the enormous size of the Red Chinese Army. Again, this perception of possible utility to the United States is a dangerous error.

First, the Red Chinese Army is a logistically deficient area based force with virtually no mobility.*

Second, there are both a vast desert and impenetrable mountains between the USSR and China. The Chinese could not maintain supply lines across this terrain except in the totally implausible event that the Soviets agreed that China itself would be treated as a sanctuary—as we did in the Korean War.

Third, Soviet forces in the Far East are in fundamentally the same posture they were in during World War II when Russia *refused* to enter the war against Japanese forces in China. Soviet Far Eastern forces, as then, are now essentially a strategic reserve for Europe, the Middle East, and other theaters.

Finally, the People's Republic of China (PRC) is a Communist dictatorship established almost entirely through Soviet assistance. The PRC has killed more than 40 million of its own people, has fostered recent genocide (3 million murdered) in Cambodia, and, as a blood drenched tyranny, has virtually nothing in common with the Western democracies.

That very little has changed is evidenced by the Chinese practise of the summary killing of dissidents, forced abortions, and the recent decision to censor even their guest, President Reagan, when he tried to tell the Chinese the truth about the

---

*In the 1981 mock war with North Vietnam, the Chinese Army was ineffective as an offensive force and could apparently advance only a few miles into Vietnamese territory.

Soviet Union. Even as it is very charitably characterized in the 1985 Department of State Annual Report on Human Rights, we are told that the PRC regime "usually deals swiftly and harshly [i.e. a bullet in the back of the head] with those who challenge its policies."

Communist China is, for those reasons, a very thin reed indeed on which to rest any part of the security of our free country.

Nevertheless, repeating errors we made in the 1920's and 1930's in our initial policy toward the Soviet Union during its own beginnings as an industrial nation, the United States is now providing Red China with tax-supported Export-Import Bank financing for importation of industrial technology and even for future orders for American aerospace equipment. Allied Bendix, Boeing, General Electric, Lockheed, Loral Corporation, Martin Marietta, McDonald Douglas, RCA, Rockwell International, and Textron are *all* seeking sales in the PRC. Additionally, the Reagan Administration is supporting China with intelligence satellite reconnaissance, with extremely advanced computers with anti-submarine warfare applications, and with nuclear technology. The Administration is also actively considering for Communist China the eventual delivery of two squadrons of advanced U.S. F-16 fighters.

These actions confirm Lenin's belief that the capitalists would "sell us the rope with which we will hang them."

India

In 1974, India tested a nuclear device.

India, however, has no ballistic or submarine launched nuclear missiles. India is loosely allied with the USSR and produces advanced Soviet MIG-23 and MIG-25 fighter aircraft under license.

India may have a small number of air deliverable nuclear bombs. These weapons, if they exist, have no real effect on global strategic posture, but in the hands of a pro-Soviet India they may affect the regional balance, particularly by undermining the security of neighboring Pakistan whose other principal border is with Soviet occupied Afghanistan.

158

APPENDIX VI

—*Sea Power*—

The United States is a maritime nation. Our geography dictates that fact, and it is ignored at peril.

To a large extent, the United States owes its position in history as an international power to the United States Navy. The defeat of the Barbary Pirates, the War of 1812, the Battle of Manila Bay, Midway: these events marked our progress from insular state to superpower while our commerce and flag reached every corner of the globe by sea.

The Soviet Union is a continental nation. Its interior geography on the broad Eurasian land mass dictates that fact. And the most memorable event in Russian naval history is the 1905 defeat of the Imperial Fleet by the Japanese at Tsushima.

Nonetheless, a remarkable reversal of roles appears to be underway. As the United States Navy shrinks from the 1,000 ships of the early 1970's to a few more than 500 today, the Soviet Navy expands to more than 2,000 with breathtaking speed and clear purpose. Soviet warships patrol the Gulf of Mexico and 1,800 Soviet flag vessels carry an enormous share of world trade at rates designed to force the vessels of other nations out of competition.

Today, only 600 merchant ships carry the American flag and the active U.S. Merchant Marine numbers only *12*. All Soviet flag ships, meanwhile, are designed from the keel up to have both commercial and military functions.

Similarly, while our Congress debates the purported benefits of a Prussian model General Staff best suited to the large land armies and small navies of Central Europe and Asia (and to the hierarchical mind-set of centralized dictatorial powers), the Soviet Union grants increasing independence to *its* Navy in proportion to its developing global mission.

Fortunately for the United States, the present Secretary of the Navy, John Lehman, understands the significance of our naval history, appreciates its lessons teaching the crucial value of sea power in our particular geographic circumstance, and is struggling to restore our rightful and necessary position as a maritime force. In this he has had less than the full support which would be forthcoming from an equally enlightened Congress.

While we believe, and feel some confidence in asserting, that Secretary Lehman shares our assessment that American inferiority in strategic nuclear and anti-nuclear forces (regardless of service component) must receive first corrective priority, we are also confident in his apparent judgment that unquestioned superiority in all aspects of sea power should advance simultaneously in efforts to restore security to our country and allies.

Mr. Lehman has set the modest goal of 600 battle force ships. That benchmark shows his practical skill as a public servant. As an interim step, it is wise. As a final objective, it falls short of the mark.

Given the gigantic size of the Red Army, we could never hope, nor should we attempt, to match Russia land division for land division. In land based air forces similar considerations pertain. But at sea, the world is different.

And it is at sea that American power can best and most efficiently be expressed. This central fact of national military experience must not be overlooked in the dangerous days ahead.

Acknowledgments
And Dedication

The authors are indebted to Ann Sullivan for her patience in permitting the use of her kitchen as work space at midnight and beyond, to Ann Sauer of the professional staff of the Senate Committee on Armed Services for unfailingly helpful and moderating criticism, to Nina Novak of the Washington law firm, Miles and Stockbridge, for innumerable corrections in spelling, punctuation, and grammar and for improvements in style and content, and to Timothy Dickenson for grossly undercompensated general editorial review. They have our very sincere thanks as do the many experts of national security and of science, both technical and political, on whose prior works we have so obviously and heavily relied. We recognize finally and primarily the inspiration given by the life and words of Winston Churchill, in which were and are embodied the principles and perceptions we have in this small volume imperfectly sought to emulate, and that given in greater measure by the bravest soldier and patriot we know, Bob Harris of Raleigh, North Carolina, to whom, trusting in his indulgence, we presume to dedicate this book.

About the Authors

QUENTIN CROMMELIN, JR. is a lawyer in Washington, D.C. with the firm of Vance, Joyce, Carbaugh, Huang, Fields and Crommelin. He is a member of the bar in New York and Alabama.

Mr. Crommelin was educated as an engineer at Rice University and as a lawyer at the University of Virginia. He is also a graduate of the U.S. Army Command and General Staff College.

In his civilian career, Mr. Crommelin has had extensive experience in goverment in areas involving monetary and fiscal policy, defense strategy, foreign affairs, and the Federal Judiciary. Beginning on the staff of the late Senator James B. Allen (Democrat of Alabama), he served subsequently as counsel to various Senators on the Committee on Armed Services, as Chief Counsel of the Senate Subcommittee on Separation of Powers, and as Staff Director of the Senate Committee on the Judiciary. Mr. Crommelin also served on the President's Transition Team for the Department of Defense and the Department of Justice.

As an army reservist, he is a Special Forces Lieutenant Colonel and served overseas in armored cavalry in Vietnam and more recently as an operations officer in Honduras.

His previously published works include *A Program for Military Independence* (Captiol Hill Staff Group, 1980) which helped form a basis for the significant changes in defense planning and policy which were initiated by President Ronald Reagan in 1981.

DAVID SULLIVAN works for the United States Senate as principal national security advisor to several Republican Senators in leadership positions.

After a lengthy career at the Central Intelligence Agency where he analysed Soviet strategy and nuclear force modernization, Mr. Sullivan resigned from the Agency in 1978 to join the staff of Senator Lloyd Bentsen (Democrat of Texas). In 1981, he accepted an appointment in the Reagan Administration as a senior official of the Arms Control and Disarmament Agency, but later returned to his present position on Capitol Hill to help implement the President's defense policies in Congress.

Mr. Sullivan was educated at Harvard University (BA Cum Laude 1965) and at Columbia University where he received a Masters Degree in International Affairs.

He is a Major in the United States Marine Corps Reserve and saw active service in the Vietnam War in Marine Combat Intelligence.

His previously published works number more than twenty articles and books on National Security and include *The Bitter Fruit of SALT: A Record of Soviet Duplicity* and *The Fatal Flaws of SALT II.*